To:

_____

From:

_____

Date:

_____

God's Call
to a
Deeper Life

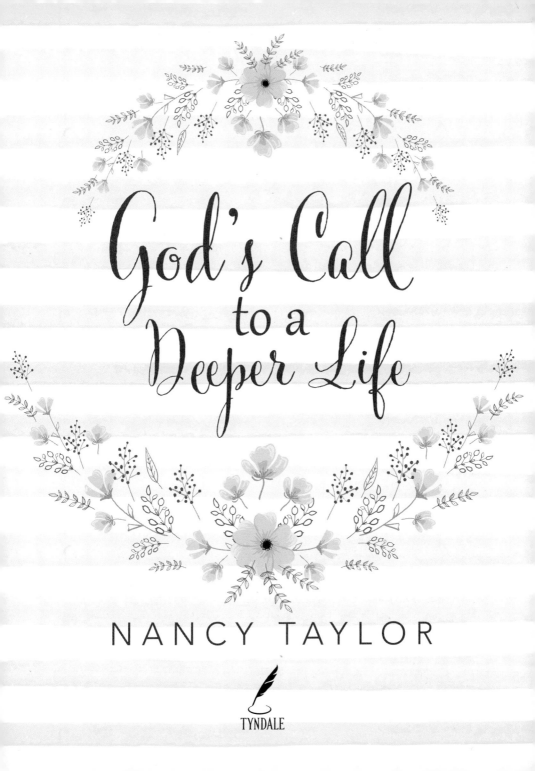

NANCY TAYLOR

TYNDALE

God's Call to a Deeper Life: Unveiling and embracing the depths of his love

© 2017 by Tyndale House Publishers, Inc.,
with permission of Three Streams Publishers, Ltd. All rights reserved.
Visit Tyndale online at www.tyndale.com.

© Copyright 2017 Three Streams Publishers, HK.

Designed by Three Streams Publishers Ltd.

Images used under license from Shutterstock.com

Written by Nancy Taylor
Visit Nancy online at www.NancyTaylorWrites.com.

Scripture quotations are taken from the *Holy Bible*, New Living Translation,
copyright © 1996, 2004, 2015 by Tyndale House Foundation.
Used by permission of Tyndale House Publishers, Inc., Carol Stream, Illinois 60188.
All rights reserved.

ISBN 978-1-4964-3011-3

Printed in China

25 24 23 22 21 20 19
8   7   6   5   4   3   2

Introduction

Do you ever wish the clouds would part and God would speak to you in an audible voice? Do you sometimes wonder if he really loves you? Do you read your Bible but at times find it dry because you can't figure out what God is trying to tell you, or how the words on the page apply to your daily life?

This book is for you. The truth is, God does speak to you—all the time! Sometimes he speaks indirectly through nature or through circumstances or through a still, small voice, but most often and most directly he speaks through his Word, the Bible. On every page he communicates his character and his will for you. The problem is, it can be difficult to figure out what God is trying to say and how it all relates to real life. That gap—between your heart and the eternal, unchanging words written in the Bible—is what this book is intended to bridge.

I hope that as these passages are paraphrased and expressed personally, you will hear God speaking them directly to you, from his heart to yours. I trust you will grasp his unfailing love for you; his passion that you be made holy, just as he is holy; his plan to bring salvation to the whole world and to your world. And I hope you will receive his gentle prodding to take the next step in figuring out where you fit into his plan to rescue sinners.

Among all the good books that teach us how to pray Scripture back to God, may this little book help you listen as God speaks to you and answers your heart's cries.

How to Use This Book

On our good days, we can read a passage of Scripture and immediately hear God speaking to us. We're in tune with his voice and eager to respond to his message. On our bad days, we feel as though we've read it all before. Nothing jumps out at us. God seems silent. Our hearts feel dry and cold.

Of course, we know God doesn't change. And we believe every word in the Bible is inspired—breathed out—by him so we can know and serve him. But some days it's just hard to hear his voice.

That's where this book comes in. It will help you read familiar Scripture passages with new eyes and hear God's heart in a new way. I've tried to take each passage and paraphrase it in God's voice so you can hear it with your heart rather than just your mind. Think of it as looking through the other side of a window—it's the same room you were just in, but now you see it from a different perspective.

My hope is that you'll read the Scripture passage listed from your

Bible, then read my personalized paraphrase of it. As you read, you may be inspired to write your own paraphrase or personal application—pull out your journal and record what God is speaking to your heart. Scripture is the only inerrant Word of God. My goal is simply to help you open your mind and heart to hear what God wants to say to you through his Word. Think of this book as a starting point for applying Scripture personally. Ask God to illuminate the Bible for you as you read it. He will always answer that prayer!

I've started with the Psalms because that is the prayer book of the Bible. As you pray words to God, listen for him to speak life-giving words back. Following that, we'll cover a few other Old Testament passages, then Jesus' words in the Gospels, and finally the Epistles and Revelation. Through it all, there is one consistent voice of God: saving, helping, keeping, and loving us to the end.

January

1

PSALM 1

They are like trees planted along the riverbank, bearing fruit each season. Their leaves never wither, and they prosper in all they do.

– Psalm 1:3

Dear child, if you want to live a blessed life, stay away from people who are bad influences. Don't listen to their advice or follow their ways or laugh at their jokes. One day the wicked will be swept away. They have no lasting legacy. They will be forgotten, and no one will mourn their passing. Don't be like them.

Instead, delight in me. That is true blessedness—deep soul happiness. Read my Word and chew on it in your mind. Memorize it, hiding it in your heart. Then you will be like a tree planted beside the water, fruitful and full of abundant life. New growth will spring up from the branches you thought were dead. Dreams and talents you have given up on will spring back to life. Delighting in me always brings forth life in your soul.

Come to me daily, trusting and listening moment by moment. Feed on my Word, for it is life. Let the Spirit's peace and joy flow through your veins and infuse everything you do with my presence and love. Rest in me, and you will both know blessedness and be a blessing to others.

We all want to live a blessed life, one of peace, joy, and deep satisfaction in the Spirit. This psalm tells us the secret to that kind of existence—plant your life in God, giving him control, and he will give back to you far more than you can imagine.

PSALM 2

Now then, you kings, act wisely! Be warned, you rulers of the earth!
Serve the LORD with reverent fear, and rejoice with trembling.

– Psalm 2:10-11

Rulers plot and rage against me. Leaders set themselves up against my dominion. People try to resist my purposes. It's funny, really—as if a mere human can have his or her way and prevail against me, the Almighty.

I have set up my true King—Jesus, the anointed one. He has the rule and authority over all the earth. At the right time he will bring evil rulers to justice and tear down nations that set themselves up in opposition to me.

Because you know this truth about the future, serve me reverently. Rejoice in all the good things in your life, but acknowledge that everything you have comes from me. Take refuge in me, not in the powers of this world, which are quickly passing away. I am the eternal King. Rest under my authority and all will be well with you, for I am the one who has all power for all time.

It is so foolish to try to rebel against the God who created us, the one who holds the universe together and controls it with a word. Yet so often we do. Choose this day to take refuge in God and rest in his plans for you.

January

3

PSALM 3

You, O Lord, are a shield around me; you are
my glory, the one who holds my head high.

– Psalm 3:3

When your enemies rise against you, trust in me. When people say I can't save you, trust in me. When you're desperate and feel alone, trust in me. Each day, each moment, trust in me.

I am your refuge. I surround you like a shield, protecting you from every danger. I lift you up and give you courage to face your troubles. There is no need to fear—I am your warrior and helper. I will stand against injustice, and I will save you. Cry out to me, and I will answer.

Rest in my care for you. Go to sleep each night in peace, knowing that I never sleep and I am working, even as you rest, to bring good to you. When you awake, you can continue to cling in faith to my sustaining love for you. From the first light of dawn to the blackness of night and every minute in between, trust me to use my limitless power for your good.

Whatever you are facing today, whoever your enemies are, God is bigger. Trust in his power to save you from every danger and sustain you through every battle.

PSALM 4

*You can be sure of this: The LORD set apart the godly
for himself. The LORD will answer when I call to him.*

– Psalm 4:3

When you call to me, I will answer. I hear and respond to every prayer, every sigh, every tear, and I will relieve your distress. Those who follow me and trust in me—who steadfastly cling to my love no matter what—have my ear.

The more you speak to me and listen to me, the more you will realize that you don't need to take revenge against those who wrong you. I will fight your battles for you. Trust me to deal with the sins of others—you just concern yourself with your own actions, making sure they are right.

As you trust in me, I pour out my goodness on you. The light of my face shines on you, the full force of my holiness and love, and my gaze brings more joy than anything the world can offer. Best of all, I give you my peace. You can go to sleep knowing I will keep you safe and arise each morning with the joyful satisfaction of a right relationship with me.

True peace comes from being reconciled to God. Each day we can clear away all our sin and every barrier we have put between ourselves and God. All we have to do is confess our sin, and he will forgive us and shine the light of his love in our hearts.

PSALM 5

Let all who take refuge in you rejoice; let them sing
joyful praises forever. Spread your protection over them,
that all who love your name may be filled with joy.

– Psalm 5:11

I hear you. I hear your groaning and crying and anguished prayers. You feel as if I'm distant, but the truth is that as you pray, morning and evening and every moment in between, I am bending down close to listen to you. I love to hear your prayers.

I do not delight in wickedness; I hate boasting and lies. But I am full of love, and anyone who wishes may draw near to me. I will lead you along my righteous paths when you seek me. I will straighten the road before you and show you which way you should go—all you need to do is ask.

The liars and deceivers will be caught in their own traps. But you, and anyone who comes to me for refuge, will be filled with joy. I will protect you. I will be a shield around you, and my favor will rest on you.

God invites us into his presence. When we seek him, he spreads his protection over us and crowns us with his favor. These are great promises that can prompt us to praise God no matter what circumstances may be causing us to groan.

PSALM 6

Return, O Lord, and rescue me. Save me because of your unfailing love.

– Psalm 6:4

I hear your cries for mercy, and I will be merciful to you. Feel me pour out my grace on you. Sense my healing hand as I reach down to soothe your troubled soul. My presence brings peace and calm even in the moments when you are frightened and in pain. Lean into me and I will wash over you with my peace.

I am the deliverer who saves you—that is my name, and my reputation is at stake. When you weep, I weep with you. When you hurt, I hurt for you. You are never alone in your suffering.

But I also know the bigger picture, the end of the story, and you can trust that I am working out everything for your good. In the end, everything will be okay because I am in control and I am good. All that I do is for your eternal good. Look at my character, look at all the times I have been faithful in the past, and trust that I am working out everything you're worried about today. Leave it in my hands and rest in the knowledge that I'm in control.

God is in the business of saving his people. He saves us from our sin, and he also saves us from the things that trouble our souls. On those days when you are weary with grief, know that God's love for you is unfailing, unflagging, and unaltered by your sin or your circumstances.

January

7

PSALM 7

*I will thank the LORD because he is just; I will
sing praise to the name of the LORD Most High.*

– Psalm 7:17

Take refuge in me, for I will save you from the people who are chasing you to destroy you. I won't let them tear you apart. See, I am rising up to defend you! I will judge evil and bring an end to injustice. I am the Lord, the righteous and just. I will save you; just stand still and let me form a shield around you.

Look! I am preparing to do battle against the evil in the world. Those who harm my precious children will fall into their own traps. Their mischief and lies will turn on their own heads. Justice will come, in my time. Wait and see—I am making all things right. Trust my plan and rest in my safe arms. I will save and protect you from all harm, for you are my precious child and I am your strong warrior.

Like any good father, our heavenly Father rises up to the defense of his children. When we are beaten down by the evil in the world, the Lord of Heaven's Armies is on our side, defending us from every one of Satan's schemes. And he has won the battle.

PSALM 8

O Lord, our Lord, your majestic name fills the
earth! Your glory is higher than the heavens.

– Psalm 8:1

My glory shines out from the heavens over all the earth. My majesty is visible in everything I have made. Think of the perfection and beauty of a tiny baby—even they praise me in their weakness, and my enemies are silenced.

Gaze into the night sky and contemplate my greatness. I put each star in place and call them by name. All of creation praises me, for each molecule and atom was formed by my hand. Everything you see and touch and experience I crafted out of nothing. Marvel at my great power.

Yet I care for you. I have numbered each hair on your head and each day of your life. I gave you a place of honor in my creation—just under the angels. I have given you a purpose and meaningful work: to care for my creation. Come, join with me in spreading my glory among the nations.

This beautiful nature poem is an invitation to praise God for everything he has made. Today, spend some time just sitting in his presence and contemplating the wonders of his creation. Let the beauty of all God has made lift your heart in praise.

PSALM 9

Those who know your name trust in you, for you,
O LORD, do not abandon those who search for you.

– Psalm 9:10

Count and recount my wonderful deeds. Think of all the ways I have been faithful through the generations. Be glad, rejoice, and sing my praises.

Your enemies mysteriously turned back—that was me working on your behalf. I am the righteous judge who sits enthroned in heaven, and everything I do is just. In the end, I will make all things right. Evil nations will be blotted out and evil deeds will be judged.

I am your stronghold. Run to me in times of trouble, and I will welcome you and hold you in my loving, strong arms. I never forsake those who love me. I am your safe place, a mighty fortress in the midst of all that frightens you and a warm home when you feel lost. Let me hold you and show you my love as you rest in my protection.

This psalm lists some of God's miraculous deeds and praises God for who he is. Add to it all the ways God has shown his faithfulness to you. How have you seen him work powerfully on your behalf?

PSALM 10

Lord, you know the hopes of the helpless.
Surely you will hear their cries and comfort them.

– Psalm 10:17

Dear one, I know all things. I know you are in despair—that you think I'm not listening. I know the terrible things that are happening, the unthinkable evil in the world. I know people are arrogant and greedy. They deny my very existence.

I also know the end from the beginning. One day I will make all things right. I am the helper of the fatherless, the just ruler for the oppressed, the defender of the defenseless. Trust me—I am working my purposes even now, even through the evil around you.

In the meantime, when the world feels upside down, know that I am listening. I do care. That's why I came into the world: to experience all the things you experience and to die so I can redeem the evil. Those wicked, evil people are made in my image too, and because of my patience in judging the world, some of them will repent and be transformed. Yes, I can change the worst sinners into saints. Trust me, I am at work, and you are not alone. Let me work out my plan while you rest in my arms.

This psalm asks honest questions, things we are not always bold enough to say to God, even if we are thinking them. Today, spend time in honest prayer and tell God what's on your heart. Then praise God for being good and just, even if you don't get answers to all your questions.

PSALM 11

The LORD is in his holy Temple; the LORD still rules from heaven.

– Psalm 11:4

Are you frightened? Do you feel alone? Does it seem as though the world is falling apart? Do you feel like the foundations of your world are crumbling beneath you? Come to me. I am your refuge, your safe place. Fly to me and nestle in like a bird fleeing to its mountain nest. You are safe and loved.

I see everything that happens on the earth. Evil people are after you—they want to destroy my people and ruin my reputation. But I am in my holy temple. My throne in heaven stands firm forever. I see their evil plots and will bring them to justice.

I also see you. I see your love for me. Because you are seeking me with your whole heart, you will find me. I will show myself to you and protect you in my loving, strong embrace.

Sometimes when we are in trouble we turn to friends, teachers, counselors, or our favorite coping mechanism before we turn to God. Next time you're in trouble, turn first to God, fleeing to him like a bird to its nest.

PSALM 12

*The LORD's promises are pure, like silver
refined in a furnace, purified seven times over.*

– Psalm 12:6

You are surrounded by so many empty words—the lying, the flattering, the boasting. The hypocrisy and flattery and double-talk. People speak the evil and deceit that is in their heart.

Tune out the world and listen to my words, so pure and so unlike the endless deceitful blustering of the wicked. My words—my revelation of myself to you—are like silver refined seven times. Utterly pure. Right. True. Holy.

I will keep you. I will guard you from the terrors on every side. I will protect you from the foulness the world spews out. And afterward I will bring you to glory. Let me speak these words of peace and truth to your heart this day. Then go forth and speak my truth to others.

Each successive generation thinks it has hit rock bottom in terms of godlessness and evil, and then the next generation manages to find a new low and descend to it. God promises to guard and protect his own as they stand for truth and light in a wicked culture.

PSALM 13

*Turn and answer me, O L*ord *my God!*
Restore the sparkle to my eyes, or I will die.

– P s a l m 1 3 : 3

Take courage, dear one. I have not forgotten you. I am not hiding from you. These days of deep sorrow will not last forever. The enemy of your soul will not have the last word.

I will shine my light on you. I will restore the sparkle to your eyes. I will save you, for my very reputation depends on it. Trust in my steadfast, forever love. Let your heart rejoice in my salvation even though everything around you is falling apart.

There is always reason to have courage and joy, for you are my child and I have redeemed you. One day you will look back and say, "The Lord has dealt bountifully with me. See what amazing things he has done!" Trust that day is coming, and live in hope.

Some days we really need God to restore the sparkle to our eyes. Nothing does that better than expressing our confidence in God's care for us. As we focus on his bountiful blessings, we gain perspective and find a reason to sing even in the darkness.

PSALM 14

The LORD looks down from heaven on the entire human race;
he looks to see if anyone is truly wise, if anyone seeks God.

– Psalm 14:2

I am searching the earth to see who seeks me, who obeys me. So many people are corrupt and chase after idols. They oppress my people, devouring them like a tasty breakfast. They wouldn't even think of praying to me, for they deny my existence. Their deeds are truly abominable, and they don't even care.

But you—you seek after me. Look for me in your circumstances and you will see that I am at work in your life and in your generation. I am with you and I am for you. You can take refuge in me, for I will bring you salvation and restore you to a life of abundant blessing. All you have to do is seek me, and you will find me.

This psalm ends with a statement of longing for God to save his people from the corruption of the world. Of course, we know that God already has! We can rejoice and be at peace, knowing that Jesus has saved us from the wickedness around us and the wickedness in our own hearts.

PSALM 15

Who may worship in your sanctuary, LORD?
Who may enter your presence on your holy hill?

– Psalm 15:1

My child, do you wish to be close to me? Then walk blamelessly and do what is right. Speak truth in your heart, and watch it flow out into truthful words. Do right to your neighbor. Hate evil and honor those who love the Lord. Be steadfast and honest.

This is the way to live a life of integrity, a life that pleases me. If you live this way, no one will be able to speak against you, for your righteous life will speak for itself. When you slip up—and you will—simply return to me. Run back into my arms, for they are flung wide to embrace you with love and forgiveness and to help you start again.

Sometimes we become so familiar with God that we think we deserve to enter his presence. The truth is, we are only worthy to ascend his holy hill through the blood of Jesus. We can enter into his presence boldly, but we must also do so humbly, knowing we can't be there on any merit of our own.

PSALM 16

I said to the Lord, "You are my Master!
Every good thing I have comes from you."

– Psalm 16:2

Take refuge in me. I will keep you safe. There is no good apart from me. Those who run after other gods heap upon themselves sorrow after sorrow. I don't accept their prayers and acts of service because they aren't truly serving me—they are serving only themselves.

But you delight in me, and I delight in you. I am your table of blessing and your place of pleasant rest. The inheritance I have saved for you is beautiful. Each day I counsel you and instruct you. As long as you set your life's compass by me, your true north, you will always find the right path.

Therefore, rejoice. Dance and sing because you are loved and you are safe. No matter what happens in this life, you can rest in the knowledge that just as I raised Jesus from the dead, so also you shall be raised to eternal life. In the meantime, follow the path I have set before you. Dwell in my presence, for that is where true joy is found.

Following false gods and idols always brings sorrow, but following God brings joy unending. Use the psalmist's list of ways God shows his goodness to inspire your own list. To what pleasant land has he brought you? What wonderful inheritance is yours?

PSALM 17

*I am praying to you because I know you will
answer, O God. Bend down and listen as I pray.*

– Psalm 17:6

Come into my presence and tell me all about your problems. Be honest with me, laying bare your soul before me. Nothing you say will surprise me or shock me, because I know all your thoughts before you even think them and I am aware of all the minute details of what concerns you. But I still like to hear it from you, so call to me. I will bend down and incline my ear to listen as you pour out your heart to me.

You are the apple of my eye, my pride and joy. Nestle close under the shadow of my wings, for I love it when you draw close to me. Hide here from all the people who lurk around wishing you harm and all the evils that lie in wait for you. See how I rise up and subdue everything that threatens to bring you harm. Draw close to me, and I will keep you safe.

Everlasting joy will be yours as you gaze on my face each day of your life—both now and when you awake from the sleep of death and see me face-to-face. This is true satisfaction, sweet fellowship with me now and through eternity.

Sometimes what we need most is a listening ear. God always listens to us, and the responses he gives us are always the truth. Next time life gets overwhelming, let God be your listening ear, as well as your voice of love, acceptance, and truth.

January 18

PSALM 18:1-24

The LORD is my rock, my fortress, and my savior;
my God is my rock, in whom I find protection. He is
my shield, the power that saves me, and my place of safety.

– Psalm 18:2

Come to me and call on my name when the cords of death seem to entangle you. Seek me when you are distressed and anxious; when it seems like the earth is reeling and its foundations are trembling; when you sense my anger at evil and sin; when my voice thunders over the rebellion of mankind. Anytime you are distressed, cry out to me.

I will draw you out of the waters of affliction. I will rescue you from those who seek to harm you. I will support and uphold you. Together we will go to a spacious place, a place of refreshment where you can delight in my love for you. Come, let us enjoy sweet fellowship and rest together as we draw away from the clamor of the world for a few minutes of peaceful respite.

David wrote this psalm after God delivered him from danger. Think of all the times God has helped you and saved you, and let these words guide you in expressing your thanks to him.

PSALM 18:25-50

Who is God except the LORD? Who but our God is a solid rock?

– Psalm 18:31

I am perfect and all my words prove true, so you can take refuge in me. You can trust that I am who I say I am and I will keep all my promises.

I am light. In me there is no darkness at all, not even a shadow. Let me light your path and guide you. I will show you the right path. I'm preparing it for you, smoothing it out so you can see the next step and making your feet secure so you can do what is right and fulfill my purposes for you.

Who is God but me alone? I give you strength when you are weary and set your feet on a firm path. With my help you can fight any army, overcome any hurdle, and defeat any foe. The battles I ask you to fight I have already trained you for. Put on my armor—the shield of salvation and the sword of the Spirit. Then follow me, and I will lead you in battle.

Indeed, I am the one who fights for you.

Whatever lies before you today, no matter how big the challenge or how daunting your foe, trust in God's provision and take courage in the knowledge that he is your mighty warrior. He has given you everything you need to do his will, and he will give you the strength you need to carry it out.

PSALM 19

*May the words of my mouth and the meditation of my heart
be pleasing to you, O LORD, my rock and my redeemer.*

– Psalm 19:14

Look at the sky—it declares my glory and proclaims my handiwork. Every day it speaks of my greatness, and in the night it declares my wisdom. With an artist's brush I paint the sky in beauty, for I am beautiful. Each day the sun rises and sets at my command and for my glory.

I have also revealed myself in my Word. Read it and be revived. Let it make you wise and give you joy. It is holy and true, and it will teach you to revere and worship me, which is what you were created to do.

Let me show you the path of joy, the way to live that will bring you deep satisfaction. That really is the point of my commands—to show you how life works best and to help you be what you were created to be. Read and study my Word, for in it you will find the words of life and unveil the depths of my love for you.

The works of God and the Word of God both proclaim his greatness and glory. Meditate on the way he reveals himself in nature and the way he reveals himself in his Word, and encourage others with everything you learn.

January

21

PSALM 20

*Some nations boast of their chariots and horses, but we boast
in the name of the LORD our God. Those nations will fall
down and collapse, but we will rise up and stand firm.*

– Psalm 20:7-8

You think of this as a day of trouble, but to me it is a day of victory. I have seen how you trust me, how you worship me in your heart and honor me as Lord of your life. Because you love me, I will be your protector and deliverer. This day I will help you and support you.

Align your heart with mine, submitting your will to my greater purposes, and see how I will transform your desires. Day by day I will reveal my plans to you, and you will see how they answer your heart's cries and perfectly meet your needs. You will shout with joy and hang up victory banners when you see my power displayed in your life!

Those who trust in their wealth and power to save them will collapse and fall. But you have placed your trust in the name of the Lord your God, and I will cause you to rise up and stand. When you call to me, I ride from heaven on my chariots of fire to save you with my powerful right hand.

God is the only one who can be trusted. People will fail and forsake us, but he is faithful. People will disappoint us and cause us to fall, but he makes us stand. Stake your life on God and his promises, and you will never be disappointed.

PSALM 21

*Rise up, O Lord, in all your power. With music
and singing we celebrate your mighty acts.*

– Psalm 21:13

Don't hang your head in defeat and gloom. Take joy in my strength, and as you learn to trust me enough to sing hallelujahs even in the darkness, you will grow ever stronger. Revel in the joy that is yours in me, true joy that transforms you on the inside so that you can face any sorrow with hope and peace.

Exult in your great salvation, claiming victory because I have given you the crown of life. You asked me for length of days, and I gave you true life now and for eternity. Yours is the rich blessing of sharing in the inheritance of Christ. Because you belong to him, you will reign with him in glory. His splendor and majesty rest on you, and his beauty brightens your countenance.

Trust in these promises and you will never be moved. You will stand firm in my steadfast love, rest in my strength, and praise me for my power. Let me make you glad with the joy of my presence as I speak these truths into your heart.

This psalm celebrates God's deliverance of the king. Think of all the things God has delivered you from, and praise him for his power and love.

PSALM 22

*I was thrust into your arms at my birth. You have
been my God from the moment I was born.*

– Psalm 22:10

I know you feel forsaken, as though I am far off and can't hear your cries for help. I know that day and night your soul is restless and anxious. Hear this:

I am holy. I sit enthroned on the praises of my people, so praise me! Join your voice with the generations before you who have found me to be faithful and allow the discipline of worship to lift your gaze to me. I brought you safely into this world, I have cared for you every day of your life, and I will never stop being faithful to you. I will deliver your soul from death and danger, for I am your rescuer.

I know that the outlook today seems bleak, but one day you will encourage others with stories of how I have been faithful to you. People will return to me because of the way you praise me. Take courage, trust in me, and see how I will carry you through this trial and use it for my glory.

From our very first infant cry to our final breath, God is with us. When it's hard to cling to that truth, the words of this psalm can encourage our hearts. Just as he was with the generations before us, God is with us. And one day we will declare his faithfulness to the next generation.

PSALM 23

The Lord is my shepherd; I have all that I need.

– Psalm 23:1

I am your gentle, good shepherd. I will give you everything you need. When you are tired and hungry, I will bring you to pleasant green pastures and give you rest and refreshment beside quiet streams. I will restore your weary soul.

At the right time—and not a moment sooner—I will lead you in the places you should go. My name and reputation depends on it, so you can trust that I will keep my promises to you. Sometimes you will walk through dark valleys and even face death. But you need not fear evil, for I am right beside you. I love you and will protect you from all harm.

Like a shepherd who guides his sheep with the rod and staff of gentle correction, I will lead you and comfort you. When you face enemies, I will nourish you with my Word. I will anoint you with the oil of healing and joy until you overflow with my goodness. Indeed, my goodness and mercy will pursue you all the days of your life. I will not let you go. Your forever home is with me.

Even when we are in the valley of the shadow of death, we will find comfort in God's presence. He may not always rescue us when we want to be rescued, but he is always with us, and even in the valleys he is preparing a feast of goodness and mercy for us.

PSALM 24

Who is the King of glory? The LORD of Heaven's
Armies—he is the King of glory.

– Psalm 24:10

The earth is mine—everything in it and everyone who lives on it. I am the Creator. I am the one who established the boundaries of the earth and founded it upon the seas.

Who is worthy to come before me? All those who humble themselves and receive my righteousness through Christ. You can stand in my presence with a heart washed clean and receive the blessings of righteousness and salvation and peace. You are made pure and holy not by your own good deeds, but because Christ died to impute my righteousness to you. Seek me and you will receive it.

Let my glory enter into the dark corners of your heart. I am strong and mighty, and I will fight to conquer every area of sin that you will offer up to me. I am the Lord of hosts, the King of glory. Let me in and see what I will do to heal and restore and reclaim the soul I have created and which I loved enough to die to redeem.

We can acknowledge with our heads that the earth is the Lord's, but still try to keep back a little bit of our hearts. We don't want to give up our pet sins or our seemingly harmless little pleasures. But we will never experience the fullness of God's love until we open wide the gates of our hearts and give him full control.

PSALM 25:1-13

Lead me by your truth and teach me, for you are the
God who saves me. All day long I put my hope in you.

– Psalm 25:5

Lift up your soul to me. Trust in me, for I will not let you be put to shame. Your enemies will not exult over you. Those who wait for me, who trust in me and let me fight their battles, will never have reason to be ashamed.

I am merciful and full of steadfast love. When you repent, I cast away all memory of your past sins and look on you with complete love. You can depend on my goodness and trust me to save you from your sins. I am your salvation.

When you ask for my guidance, I will show you my ways and the right path to take. Humbly seek my truth and I will teach you, for I am good to you in every way and in every moment. All my paths are steadfast love and faithfulness. Reverence me, and you will be at peace in your inmost being. Your soul will abide in well-being, for I offer to you the blessed inheritance of my love and faithfulness.

The tender, loving care of our Savior is evident in every line of this psalm. He guides us and teaches us as we seek his will. When we repent, he remembers his mercy but forgets our sin. Gaze on this great God and rejoice in his covenant love for you.

January

27

PSALM 25:14-22

The LORD is a friend to those who fear him. He teaches them his covenant.

– Psalm 25:14

Because you honor me in your heart, I call you my friend. My face is turned toward you in grace. I put my unshakable covenant love on you and lead you along the right path. Fix your gaze on me, and I will rescue you.

I see that you are lonely. You think that no one can understand the sorrows you bear. The troubles of your heart weigh you down and overwhelm you. But I understand. I am with you in this pain. I bore all of that and more on the cross, and I overcame so that you can overcome.

Take heart; you are loved and forgiven. I will guard your soul and deliver you from all your enemies. Because you take refuge in me, you will not be disappointed or ashamed. I guard your soul and your life. I will redeem you and show you the purpose in your pain as you wait on me.

What a blessed thing it is to call God our friend! He is the one who saves us from our troubles and provides refuge from every danger. Today, talk to God as you would a friend and rest in the security of his love for you.

January
28

PSALM 26

Declare me innocent, O LORD, for I have acted with integrity;
I have trusted in the LORD without wavering.

– Psalm 26:1

If you live with integrity, doing what is right even when no one is watching, you will be vindicated in the end. Stay away from people who tell lies. Don't hang out with hypocrites. Instead, spend time in worship, with my people.

The true test of integrity is in your heart and in your mind. Do you trust me? Will you do right even when my commands go against popular opinion? Do you fit in better with self-righteous hypocrites or with those who are humble and contrite in spirit? Test yourself, and see if the habitation of your heart is with me, where my glory dwells, or with sinners and bloodthirsty men.

You won't fall away or fall in with the wrong crowd if you are seeking me. You are redeemed by my gracious sacrifice, so live like it! Stand firm in your faith, walk in integrity, and speak my praise. Then your way will be clear and your communion with me will be sweet and unhindered.

This psalm gives us an extended definition of integrity. Integrity is moral uprightness or unity of being. It is being just as honest and trustworthy when no one will see us as we are when everyone is looking. Note the characteristics and the rewards of living such an honest and pure life before God and others.

PSALM 27

Even if my father and mother abandon me, the LORD will hold me close.
– Psalm 27:10

I am light and salvation. You have nothing to fear, for I am your stronghold. Take courage! Do not be afraid of evildoers who seek to devour you or adversaries and foes who long to see you fail. Even if a whole army surrounds you, poised to attack, you can be confident in my protection. You will rise above your enemies and live to praise me.

Come, sit in my sanctuary. Walk boldly into my throne room and gaze on my beauty. Bring your questions to me, for I am a safe shelter. I will hide you in my tent for as long as you need a secure place, and then at the right time I will lift you up on a high rock.

I will never turn my back on you. Even if your mother and father forsake you, I will not. You will yet experience my goodness—just be patient and wait for it. Take courage and be strong, for I am coming to your aid.

The salvation we have in Christ gives us courage and security. As you read these triumphant words, meditate on all the blessings that are yours because you trust in God for salvation. Then live with confidence, free from fear, because God is your Savior.

January

30

PSALM 28

Listen to my prayer for mercy as I cry out to you for help,
as I lift my hands toward your holy sanctuary.

– Psalm 28:2

In your day of trouble, cry out to me. I am a rock, safe and strong, but I am not deaf to your cries. I hear your pleas for mercy. I love it when you cry to me for help and lift up your hands in praise, surrender, or helpless desperation.

Evil people will one day get what they deserve—to them I am the judge. But for you, I am strength and mercy. I am your shield, the one you can trust to protect you. Exult in me and sing songs of thanks, for I am your strength and your saving refuge.

You do not have to be strong—bring me your weakness and I will show my strength through you. I am your gentle shepherd, and the moment you cry out to me, I lift you on my shoulders and carry you to safety. Let me carry you through all of life's difficulties. You can trust that I will bring you safely to the other side.

No matter what your mood is, whether you are desperate, joyful, or somewhere in between, God longs to hear from you. Bring him your pleas for mercy. Come to him in triumphant worship. Sing songs of praise and utter groanings too deep for words. God listens to it all, and he will be your saving refuge.

PSALM 29

Honor the LORD for the glory of his name.
Worship the LORD in the splendor of his holiness.

– P s a l m 2 9 : 2

The angels in heaven praise my glory and strength. They worship my name for the splendor of my holiness. My voice is over the waters, hovering in creative power. My glory thunders out over the seas in power and majesty. Storms come and go at my bidding. Huge trees break with a word from my lips. Great nations are tamed at my command.

I am enthroned over all things, the forever King, yet I care for you. Even to the number of hairs on your head, I know every detail about you. That is how much I love you. I give you strength to face any difficulty, and the blessing of my peace rests upon you.

Revel in this truth: the great King over all loves you deeply—even to the cross. Since I am on your side, you have nothing to fear. My great power is for you.

God is so great and mighty that sometimes we lose sight of the fact that he is also madly in love with us. As you glorify him for his majesty, revel in the blessing of peace that he offers you. The Creator God came to earth as a baby and died on a cross to save you.

PSALM 30

His anger lasts only a moment, but his favor lasts a lifetime!
Weeping may last through the night, but joy comes with the morning.

– Psalm 30:5

Are you in trouble? Do your enemies taunt you? Cry to me for help. I will draw you out of your trials and silence those who would do you harm. I will bring healing and restoration to all the broken places.

My anger lasts only a moment, but my favor rests on you forever. Though you may weep for the night, joy is coming with the morning light. Hang on to this hope. The struggles are there to make you cry out to me. They remind you of how much you need me, of who I am and who you are—my beloved child.

Rejoice that your mourning can be turned to dancing. Your guilt replaced with gladness. Your silent tears traded for shouts of praise. Every spiritual blessing is already yours in Christ, so claim your joy and peace today.

When troubles overwhelm us, we often lose perspective. All we can see is the magnitude of our problems, and it feels as though they will never end. But God gives us a long-term view of things: our troubles last only a moment when compared to the eternal joy that awaits us.

PSALM 31:1-8

I entrust my spirit into your hand.
Rescue me, LORD, for you are a faithful God.

– Psalm 31:5

I see your affliction and the distress of your soul. Your fear is not hidden from me. Come, take refuge in me and you will never be put to shame. I will deliver you from all your troubles. I bend low to listen to your cries for help, then I wrap my strong arms around you and pick you up. Refuge and fortress are my name.

See, I have placed your feet on level ground. Surrender to this path I have you on. Walk with me in joy and peace. I lead you and guide you because you are mine and I have promised it. When you committed yourself to me, I placed my faithful love on you forever. Freely rejoice in my steadfast love, and walk this path with courage and joy because I am with you.

Entrusting ourselves to God means resting in his plans for us and embracing the path he's put us on—even if our circumstances are not what we would choose. No matter what is going on around us, we can entrust ourselves to the faithful God who loves us and is our refuge in times of trouble.

PSALM 31:9-24

I am trusting you, O LORD, saying,
"You are my God!" My future is in your hands.

– P s a l m   3 1 : 1 4 - 1 5

Dear soul, I see you withering with grief. I hear your sighs and groaning. I know you feel like your life is poured out and your bones are wasting away. You are not forgotten. I see you, I love you, and I am with you. Remember, I poured my life out as a drink offering for you at the cross. You can trust me because I've endured it all and paid the price to save you.

All the seasons of your life are in my hands—your past, your future, and everything in between. It is all in my loving hands and under my power, so you have nothing to fear. I will take care of you.

Take cover here under the shelter of my presence, and I will shower my abundant goodness on you. I will hide you from your enemies and show you my steadfast love. Be strong. Take heart. Have courage. Wait on me, and I will deliver you.

This psalm promises us that even if we are in such distress that our bones are wasting away, there is great goodness stored up for us. Take courage as you think about that promise, and run to the safety of God's sheltering presence.

February

4

PSALM 32

Oh, what joy for those whose disobedience
is forgiven, whose sin is put out of sight!

– P s a l m   3 2 : 1

You are blessed. When nothing is going right and everything that could go wrong has gone wrong, you are still blessed because you are forgiven. Your sins are covered by my blood. I don't count them against you because I already paid the penalty on your behalf.

When you harbor sin, hiding it and deceiving people, it eats you up inside. Acknowledge your sin. Uncover it before me—I know all about it anyway. Confess, and I will forgive you, no matter what you've done. You can have that weight of shame lifted from your shoulders. You can be free of it forever. All you need to do is repent before me.

So don't be stubborn. Hide yourself in me, the one who knows everything about you and loves you anyway. Let my steadfast love envelop you. Rejoice in who I am and what I have done. Be glad and shout for joy because you are forgiven.

We don't always think of confession as a joy. After all, it takes great humility to tell someone about something we are ashamed of. But it is through confession and repentance that we can find forgiveness, and that is indeed great joy. Let God be your hiding place by confessing your sin to him.

PSALM 33:1-11

Let the whole world fear the LORD, and let everyone stand in awe of him.

– Psalm 33:8

Shout for joy! Wear your praises like a garment—put them on each day, and let praise and thanks be the characteristic posture of your soul. Sing, make music, shout a new song.

If you don't feel like praising me, if your circumstances aren't making you thankful, consider my character. That is reason enough to praise me all day long. I am good and faithful, and all my words prove true. I love righteousness and justice. The earth overflows with evidence of my steadfast love. I made the heavens with a word and filled them with a breath. All the waters of the sea are contained in my storehouses.

Let the earth fear me. Nations may seem all-powerful, but I am sovereign over all things. One word from me and they will be no more, for the plans of my heart stand forever. I am the sovereign Creator who loves you and is working everything for your good.

The God we serve is the creator of all things, and his plans stand firm forever. Spend time today praising God for his greatness.

February
6

PSALM 33:12-22

Let your unfailing love surround us, LORD, for our hope is in you alone.

– Psalm 33:22

I see into the heart of each person. I look down from the throne room of heaven and know every detail about the people I have made. I see you, and I know you honor me in your heart. Therefore, I will deliver you. I am your helper who sees your need even before you do and who is already rising up to meet it. I am your shield, protecting you from dangers you can't even see.

Other people place their hope in power and wealth, or in the security of earthly authorities. But in the day of trouble none of those things can help them. Everything will come crashing down around them.

But you have nothing to fear because you have placed your hope in me, and I am a strong anchor for your soul. Be glad because you trust in the one who is completely trustworthy. Wait for me—I always come through. Hope in me, for my steadfast love rests on you forever.

Our hope and security come from the knowledge that God is watching over us. Nothing else can save us or protect us, only God. Thank God for his unfailing love that surrounds you and shields you from every danger.

PSALM 34:1-10

*Taste and see that the LORD is good. Oh, the
joys of those who take refuge in him!*

– Psalm 34:8

When life is going well, bless my name. When things are falling apart and nothing seems good, that also is the time to bless my name. I am worthy of praise all the time, in all circumstances, because I am good all the time. My ways are perfect, and in the end I will make everything right. So praise me for that future hope even on the darkest days.

When you seek me, I will deliver you from all your fears—whether the threat is real or imagined. Look to me and your face will radiate with my peace and joy. You are safe because my angels have set up camp all around you, protecting and saving you.

Those who love me lack no good thing. If something is good for you, you will have it! Sometimes in your limited perspective you think something is good that isn't. Trust me. I know what is best, and I will do nothing less for you than the best. Come and taste my goodness.

God's goodness is something we can taste and see—it is all around us, if we will just open our eyes to see it and our hands to receive it. What would you do differently today if you really believed that those who trust in the Lord lack no good thing? Live like you believe it!

February 8

PSALM 34:11-22

The righteous person faces many troubles,
but the LORD comes to the rescue each time.

– Psalm 34:19

D ear child, do you want to live a good life? The secret is to revere me, honoring me in your heart and living a life of obedience. Watch what you say; don't speak evil or tell lies. Turn away from wickedness and do good. Run after peace like it's the greatest treasure you could have.

Then I will hear your cries. I turn my face toward those who follow me, but I turn away from those who pursue wrong. Cry out to me; I will hear you and save you. In all your troubles, I will be near to help you.

Following me will not save you from every difficulty—my children sometimes suffer greatly—but I am close to you in your sorrow. When you are brokenhearted, I am especially near. And I will keep you safe. The day of trouble will crush those who don't have me to lean on, but for those who love me it is a day of redemption. I am your refuge, and I will save and preserve you and establish you on firm ground.

God doesn't promise us a trouble-free life. In fact, Jesus told us we would have many troubles in this life (John 16:33). But he also promised that he has overcome them all. Praise God for his protection even in the midst of difficulty, and cry out to him to rescue the brokenhearted.

PSALM 35

I will rejoice in the LORD. I will be glad because he rescues me.

– Psalm 35:9

You want me to fight your enemies, to be your warrior. And you do indeed have an enemy: Satan and his forces want to steal and destroy and kill. They work for your destruction, accusing and tempting you at every turn.

But I am your shield. I carry out justice, for I *am* perfect justice. I am the God of all salvation, the righteous and victorious King. I defend the afflicted and punish evil.

Therefore, you can rest. You have a divine advocate fighting for you, so you can give up the struggle. Leave your case in my hands. Let me quiet your soul with a single word. Rejoice in my salvation, for there is none like me—strong and holy and full of mercy. Those who boast in themselves will be brought to shame, but those who magnify me will be vindicated. One day soon you will shout with delight and joyfully tell others how I have brought justice where there was evil, how I have done good to you.

Many times we need more than anything for God to show up, for him to rescue the helpless and bring justice to the oppressed. He has promised that he knows all about our troubles and he will work justice and give us peace.

February
10

PSALM 36

Your unfailing love, O LORD, is as vast as the heavens;
your faithfulness reaches beyond the clouds.

– Psalm 36:5

Those caught up in habitual sin get more and more brazen. They think they will never get caught. Even as they lie in bed, they plot more evil. They have no shame.

But I am full of steadfast love. My care for you reaches to the heavens, my faithfulness to the clouds. My righteousness stands like the mountains, and all that I am is devoted to saving and rescuing you. Come, rest under my wings. Feast on my abundance. Drink of my delights, for I am the fountain of life. Apart from me there is no true life, but with me is life abundant and full.

My steadfast love will cling to you. I will protect you from all dangers and bring you safely to heaven, your true home, where you can feast on my delights and rest in my presence forever.

We all have a choice in life: Will we pursue sin or righteousness? Will we go our own way or choose God's way? If we choose to trust in the Lord, he will shelter us under his wings and pour out his unfailing love on us.

February
11

PSALM 37:1-7

Take delight in the Lord, and he will give you your heart's desires.

– Psalm 37:4

Don't worry about the people who seem to have it all, despite the fact that they are cheaters and unjust and wicked. Don't fret over them or be jealous of what they have. One day their riches will dissolve like dust.

Choose the better way: trust me. Do what is good. Be faithful in the places to which I have called you. Delight yourself in me and allow me to give you the desires of your heart—the desires I have birthed within you. Commit your way to me, trusting in me alone, and your righteousness will shine out.

Be still before me. Wait patiently for me to speak and act. My timetable is not the same as yours—it's better, because it's perfect. So wait on me, breathe in my presence, and watch me make everything right in the end.

Spending our lives chasing after wealth and success will only lead to emptiness. But if we trust the Lord and commit ourselves to him, we will have the kind of prosperity that really matters: peace.

February
12

PSALM 37:8-40

The LORD directs the steps of the godly. He delights in
every detail of their lives. Though they stumble, they will
never fall, for the LORD holds them by the hand.

– Psalm 37:23-24

Don't be angry and fretful about the evil in the world. I see it; I know what's going on. People plot to kill and destroy. They borrow with no intention to repay. They do unspeakable evil. They scheme against my people. But their end is sure: Unless they turn to me in repentance and choose to follow me, they will be destroyed. They will have no part in the eternal life I offer.

But you are not like them. My imprint is in your heart, and you are evermore becoming like me. Because you have made me your stronghold, you will live with me forever.

With me you have abundant peace. I uphold you and give you my eternal inheritance. You may fall, but I always catch you. You are never forsaken, never abandoned, never condemned. Your feet do not slip. Rest in me. Wait for me. Your ways and your days are in my hand, both today and for eternity.

The hope we have in Christ is for this life as well as the next. He helps us each day now and forever.

PSALM 38

My guilt overwhelms me—it is a burden too heavy to bear.

- P s a l m 3 8 : 4

I hear every sigh, every unspoken longing, every anguished cry. I see your sinful thoughts and attitudes. I know all about the iniquities that weigh on you like a heavy burden. All of it is laid bare before me; nothing is hidden from my sight. Yet I still love you. Your friends may judge and reject you, but I will not. I see every sinful thought and the very worst of your selfishness, and still I draw near to you in love.

Others accuse you; I redeem you. Others judge; I justify through my blood poured out for your sin. Others seek your ruin; I work for your good. Others stand far off; I bring you near.

Lay yourself before me. Release all the sin you've been trying to hide. I know it anyway, and you will find great freedom in complete honesty.

Wait and rest in me. Sense my nearness. Let me speak over you words of forgiveness, acceptance, and love.

This psalm paints a vivid picture of the pain of unconfessed sin. If you have been harboring your wrongdoing, or even just glossing over what seem like "little" sins, use these words to confess and then receive God's lavish forgiveness.

February 14

PSALM 39

We are merely moving shadows, and all our busy rushing ends in nothing. . . . And so, Lord, where do I put my hope? My only hope is in you.

– Psalm 39:6-7

I know the length of your days. I am the one who knows the end from the beginning. Every one of your days is preknown and preplanned by me—even the days you wish had never happened. I've known about every event in your life from before time began. There are no surprises to me.

In the span of eternity, your life is a blip—a mist—here today, gone in an instant. Yet far from being insignificant, you are precious to me. I know everything about your life, and I am preparing you for a blessed future. I go there before you and gently lead you into it.

Therefore, you can hope in me. I am working everything out for your good and my glory. Trust that I hold the future in my loving hands, and that all the uncertainty and pain is part of my good plan. Not one moment will be wasted; I will redeem it all.

Our years on earth may be short or long, but all of us will one day pass into eternity. Let these words give you perspective and encourage you to live today in view of eternity.

PSALM 40:1-8

He has given me a new song to sing, a hymn of praise to our God. Many will see what he has done and be amazed.

– Psalm 40:3

There you were, in a deep pit, covered with slime and muck. The stench of evil and filth clung to you. But I reached down and pulled you out. I set you on firm ground, cleansed you, and clothed you in my righteousness. What a beautiful song of praise you can sing now!

Because you trusted in me and waited for me, I have blessed you. Many are the wondrous deeds I have done and continue to do for you. I think fondly of you—so many thoughts that you couldn't even name them all.

All of this is yours, yet I require so little. I want relationship. Talking and listening. Not sacrifice, but confession. Not burnt offerings, but a heart offered in love. Take one step toward me, one half turn, and I will bound toward you with open arms to enfold you in my love.

Sometimes we think we need to come before God with a list of our accomplishments or a handful of rituals. But God just wants our hearts, honest and open and offered to him in love. Will you do that today?

February
16

PSALM 40:9-17

May all who search for you be filled with joy and gladness in you.

– Psalm 40:16

Just as you have proclaimed my deliverance, not holding back from telling others about my faithfulness, so I will not restrain my mercy from you. I will pour it over you, cleansing the sewage of sin from your body with my rivers of grace. Plunge yourself deep into the fresh, cool waters of the fountain of life.

I know that you feel like you are surrounded by evil. Your own sin, mingled with the world's sin, overwhelms you and threatens to drag you into the mire. But I am your deliverer. I run to your aid, lavishing my mercy on you. I am the God who saves.

The harm others contrive against you will fall back on their own heads. They will be dishonored. But you will be glad and rejoice. You will once again proclaim my greatness because I came for you and saved you.

When troubles pile up around us, we can run to the Lord for rescue. He will save all those who search for him and will give them joy and gladness in his presence.

February 17

PSALM 41

The LORD nurses them when they are sick and restores them to health.

– Psalm 41:3

You've devoted your life to doing the right thing, and yet now you find yourself in deep suffering. This isn't what you expected. Everyone has given up on you. Even your friends think you are beyond hope. Some have even betrayed you and now seek to harm you.

They have forgotten that with me there is always hope. I delight in you, and my power to heal and save is without limit. Nothing is impossible for me. I will yet show you my grace and raise you up. The shouts you hear will not be your enemies' taunts, but your own shouts of joy. I am from everlasting to everlasting, and I will set you in my presence because you trust in me!

God is in the business of restoring what is broken. That is why we can come before him with confidence and ask him to heal us and those we love. Whether healing comes in this life or the next, he always rescues and restores those who trust him.

February

18

PSALM 42

Why am I discouraged? Why is my heart so sad? I will put my
hope in God! I will praise him again—my Savior and my God!

– Psalm 42:11

Your soul is panting, aching, longing for something. You try to fill the gaping hole with lesser things, with stuff and experiences and physical pleasure, but your soul is really panting for me. I am the only source of living water.

When you try to quench your deep spiritual thirst with earthly things, you end up depressed and distraught. Your soul is in turmoil because you want earthly things to fill the void only I can fill. Lift up your head. Remember how you used to joyfully shout with the throngs of my people.

Return to me, the living water, and drink of the fountain of life. Let me fill the deep places in your soul that are crying out to me. Hope in me, praising me even in the dark. Let my steadfast love pour over you and renew you. I will fully satisfy you if you open your soul to me and let me fill it.

Christians have no need to wallow in sadness and discouragement. God is our refuge and strength, and he is more than enough to satisfy.

February

19

PSALM 43

*Send out your light and your truth; let them guide me. Let them
lead me to your holy mountain, to the place where you live.*

– Psalm 43:3

Justice will be done. In the end, right will win and evil will be defeated.
I have promised it, and every promise of mine is as good as done. I am
holy and just, and I can do all things. Therefore, you can trust me to right
every wrong.

But that is in the future, and right now you live in a broken world.
Sometimes the evil and injustice are overwhelming. At those times, take
refuge in me. Run to me and be safe. When you're not sure what to do,
ask me. I will be your guide for every step. Follow me, and I will lead you
into my truth and light.

Don't be cast down. Hope in me and trust that you will again praise
me. Come into my presence, for there you will find holy joy and exceeding
peace. Praise me for the justice that is coming and trust me for it.

When we look only at what is going on in the world, we can
easily get discouraged. But if we gaze into the face of God, we
can watch our faith grow as we realize we can trust him to bring
justice to the earth.

February

20

PSALM 44

O God, we have heard it with our own ears—our ancestors have told us of all you did in their day, in days long ago.

– Psalm 44:1

Listen to the stories others tell of my faithfulness. I plant people in fertile ground, causing them to flourish and bear fruit. I throw down rulers and save my people with might and mercy. I delight in my people and place my crown of salvation on them. I do all of this not because they deserve it, but because I love them. Don't place your confidence in yourself, in your status or abilities or attractiveness. Place your trust in me and give me thanks.

I know you sometimes feel rejected and forgotten. You look at the suffering in the world and in your own life and wonder where I am.

Take heart! I am still on my throne. I will be faithful to you and this generation just as I have been in the past. I am the same God yesterday, today, and forever. I am working all things according to my merciful and just plan, for your good and my glory. I love you, and I am working things out. Trust me.

When life is especially difficult, it's helpful to remind ourselves of all God has done for us in the past. And if we don't have our own stories, or if we can't remember them in the darkness, we can borrow others' stories to bolster our confidence.

PSALM 45

Your royal husband delights in your beauty; honor him, for he is your lord.

– Psalm 45:11

Sing of the majesty of Christ, your bridegroom! I am a handsome prince, gracious in speech and blessed forever. I ride in majestic might, like a warrior king. But I did not come to set up an earthly kingdom. Instead, I prick people's consciences with arrows of truth so I might conquer their hearts.

My Kingdom is peace and righteousness. The fragrance of holiness follows me wherever I go, clinging to my robes of righteousness like a beautiful perfume.

Come, inhabit my heavenly palace with me forever. All you must do to share in this glory is join my bride, the church of all the saints through the ages. Renounce all others who vie for your attention and be faithful to me alone. Then you will be clothed in glorious robes and enjoy my presence for all eternity. Enter into the joy of your beloved, for you are loved.

This royal wedding psalm is applied to Christ in Hebrews 1:8-9. If we are in Christ, we are part of the church, his bride. That metaphor should help us feel loved and cherished every day of our lives.

PSALM 46

Be still, and know that I am God! I will be honored by
every nation. I will be honored throughout the world.

– Psalm 46:10

I am your refuge and strength, a very present help in trouble. When the earth melts and the mountains crumble into the sea, do not fear. Don't focus on the roaring and foaming of the waters around you. Instead, look forward to the rivers of heaven.

I am with you; therefore you will not be moved. I will keep you safe all your days and afterward bring you to glory. I am the fortress in your midst, a place of safety and security. Nations may rage, but I utter a word and they are reduced to rubble. I break their might and bring them down.

As for you, be still. Stop your fretting and striving. Ponder in your heart that I am God. Wait on me. I am working all things so that one day I will be exalted over the whole earth. Run to me and be safe while you wait for that day when I will restore all things to glorious perfection.

This beloved psalm is a victory cry when our world seems to have fallen off its axis. Our job is simple: Be still and trust God. When we do that, the mighty creator and sustainer of the universe will be our refuge.

PSALM 47

God reigns above the nations, sitting on his holy throne.

– Psalm 47:8

Clap your hands! Shout with joy! I am all-powerful and holy, worthy of your reverence and awe. I subdue nations and choose rulers. I go out in battle with a shout and a trumpet blast. I am the King on high, all-powerful and victorious in battle. I rule over all the earth. Sing praises to me, for I have won the victory! I am on my holy throne and have conquered every evil.

The battle for your soul was won at the cross. I have defeated sin and death, so they no longer have any hold on you. Now you can rest in my power, which is for you. I am the King of your heart, bending low to listen to your cries and rising up to meet your need. The earth is mine, so I can do anything. You are mine, so I will do what is best for you.

If we could just keep fresh before our eyes a vision of God reigning in victory over all things, so many of our problems would sort themselves out. He is King over all of our problems, all of our sins, all of the circumstances of our lives. And because he loves us, we can trust him to do good things for us.

PSALM 48

He is our God forever and ever, and he will guide us until we die.

– Psalm 48:14

I am your great King. I am your fortress of protection and refuge in times of trial. I dwell with my people to help them, and since everything I do is perfect, you can trust that my judgments are right. Those who do wrong, who oppress and kill and destroy, are terrified of me because they know in their hearts that their actions will be punished.

But you will live in my glorious Kingdom forever. It is a Kingdom of love and righteousness. Everyone in it is full of joy because they are near to me. There is no pain or trouble there, no crying or anguish. That is where I am leading you.

The path through this life may be rocky and difficult. You may experience deep pain. But I am with you always, guiding you to my perfect forever-Kingdom in heaven. Trust me to get you there safely and to be with you every step of the way.

In the Old Testament, God filled the Temple with his presence. Now, through the Holy Spirit, he lives in our hearts and rules over our lives. But one day he will rule over a new heaven and a new earth, a place where there is no sorrow or pain.

PSALM 49

*As for me, God will redeem my life. He will
snatch me from the power of the grave.*

– Psalm 49:15

Wealth is deceitful. People who have much think they can get away with anything. They trust in what they have to preserve them from the day of trouble. But their confidence is misplaced. No one can pay the ransom to save his own soul—only I can do that. Rich people who trust themselves and the gifts I have given them instead of trusting me to save them will die with nothing. Their wealth can't save them from death, and no one can take anything with them when they die.

Don't suffer their fate. Trust in me. I paid the price to buy back your soul from Satan's power. I have ransomed you; you are mine. Death has no power over you because you have an eternal home with me. Live for that day when you will enter my presence, storing up what lasts for eternity rather than storing up the things of earth, which quickly decay.

People who go through life only caring for the wealth they accrue or the security they find in their own accomplishments will one day find they have nothing of lasting value. They die and are forgotten. This truth should help us not be envious of what others have and remind us to focus on things that last for eternity.

PSALM 50

Giving thanks is a sacrifice that truly honors me.

– Psalm 50:23

Call me Mighty One, God the Lord, the one who speaks and the earth moves. I shine forth in perfection and beauty. I come speaking and doing, like a devouring fire or a mighty tempest. I call people and nations out and judge them.

But to you, my child, I speak covenant words. My faithful love is set on you like a seal on your heart. You are righteous and uncondemned because I am righteous and paid the price to buy back your soul from sin and death. I am your God, the one who saves you.

I don't need anything from you—after all, the whole earth is mine—but I desire your sacrifice of praise. Be thankful for all I have done for you, and don't forget my gracious deeds. Thanksgiving is the key to rightly ordering your life; it puts everything into perspective. So each day choose gratitude.

God doesn't need anything from us, but he desires our praise and thanksgiving. It's such a small sacrifice; won't you give it to him today?

PSALM 51

Create in me a clean heart, O God. Renew a loyal spirit within me.

– Psalm 51:10

I pour my mercy over you because I love you with steadfast love. Every one of your transgressions is blotted out. You are utterly cleansed from your sin.

All this abundant grace is yours because you confessed your sin and repented. You know that only I can purge the sin from your heart, so you came to me for soul healing. That humble soul-baring is the secret to obtaining a clean heart and a right spirit.

Now I will restore to you the joy you once had in your salvation. You were broken; now you can rejoice. You were weighed down by your sin, but I have lifted your head. You were hiding in sin, but now your lips are opened to declare my praise. Do you sense how loved and forgiven you are? Run in that freedom, like a young colt released from its pen!

This famous psalm of repentance offers us a model for confession. Use it to lay your heart bare before the Lord, and then receive his forgiveness with joy.

February
28

PSALM 52

I will praise you forever, O God, for what you have done. I will
trust in your good name in the presence of your faithful people.

– Psalm 52:9

Evil men plot destruction and boast of their wickedness. The lies they tell reveal that they love injustice and wrong more than good. I am justice. I will break them down and uproot them from the land of the living. Their days are numbered.

But you run to me for refuge. You trust in the abundance of my love rather than the abundance of riches. You speak truth rather than lies. Therefore you are like a lush green olive tree. You grow upright, strong in me. I nourish you from the inside out so you can bear ripe fruit to feed hungry souls.

Stand firm in the rich soil of my love for you. Remain in me and I will remain in you. As you rest in my good care for you, you will regain strength. Wait on me, patiently enduring the growing process, and I will give you everything you need to grow and flourish. Then you will praise me before others.

Wicked people boast and tell lies; those who trust in the Lord praise him and speak truth. Think about what your words say about your heart, and then meditate on James 3 and consider how to make your words better.

February
29

PSALM 53

All have turned away; all have become corrupt.
No one does good, not a single one!

– Psalm 53:3

I t is foolish to try to deny my existence, yet people do it every day. If they look around at the things I have made, their hearts will tell them that I exist. But they stubbornly ignore what their senses reveal to them.

I am looking for people who seek me, but I see so many who have fallen away. Apart from me, people plunge into sin and wrongdoing. They are corrupted and unable to do good, and one day they will be eaten up by terror.

But salvation has come to you. Rejoice and be glad, for I have come to save you. I have brought you back from the clutches of evil. Your heart is now mine, and I whisper to you, "I am here!" Each time you seek me you will find me, for I am yours and you are mine. I am encamped around you, protecting and keeping you always.

These words are quoted by the apostle Paul in Romans 3:10-12. Every person is born in the grip of sin, and our only hope of escape is to trust in Jesus to save us. When we turn to him, he will abundantly forgive.

March

PSALM 54

*I will praise your name, O Lord, for it is good. For you have rescued
me from my troubles and helped me to triumph over my enemies.*

– Psalm 54:6-7

I am the one who saves you. Run to me, your refuge and helper, when you are in trouble. I will defend you with my power and might.

I hear your prayers. I know that ruthless enemies have risen up against you. These godless people are really coming against me, because you are mine. I will turn the evil they plan for you back on them. One day they will receive justice for their wickedness.

I will uphold your life and deliver you. Final victory has already been achieved at the cross. It is finished. Rest in the assurance that I am working everything out, and know that you can thank me as if your deliverance has already happened—it is that sure.

Every day of our lives we rely on God for life and protection from evil. Use this psalm to pray against the enemies you can't see, the forces of darkness, and then rest in God's care for you and his final victory over evil.

PSALM 55

Give your burdens to the LORD, and he will take care
of you. He will not permit the godly to slip and fall.

– Psalm 55:22

My ear is attuned to your voice. I hear every plea for mercy, every restless moan. I know you feel oppressed and in danger, anguished at heart by the terrors of death and the betrayal of those you trusted.

Fly away like a dove and nestle in close to me. Find refuge in me. Take shelter in my embrace. I will keep you safe from the raging tempest that swirls around you.

Keep calling on me, morning and night. I am the only one who can redeem you and bring you safely through this battle. Many may rise against you, but I am greater. Cast all your burdens on me, and I will sustain you. I never allow those who trust in me to be moved. You are safe in my hand.

The worst pain is personal betrayal, when someone we love and trust turns against us. Jesus understood that pain firsthand when Judas handed him over to his enemies to be killed. When we face the deepest pain imaginable, God is there. Cry out to him and rest in his care.

PSALM 56

I trust in God, so why should I be afraid? What can mere mortals do to me?

– Psalm 56:11

People may trample on you and oppress you. There will be enemy attacks, battles against the forces of darkness and sometimes even against flesh and blood. When you are afraid, you can put your trust in me. I am trustworthy, always keeping my promises and loving you with a steadfast love. Therefore, you do not need to be afraid. No one can snatch you out of my hand, and no harm can come to you without my consent.

I have kept count of your sleepless nights. Every tear you have shed, I keep in a bottle. Every sigh is recorded in my book. I love you, and I have carried every one of your sorrows in my heart.

But that's not the whole story. These sorrows are but a single snapshot in the span of eternity. I have delivered your soul from death. I keep your feet from falling and help you walk in new life. Your sorrows are not wasted, for they draw you closer to me, the life-giver and the light of the world. Walk with me and you will be walking in the light of life.

What a comforting thought it is that God stores our tears in a bottle. He cares about everything that concerns us. On days of sorrow, give your emotions to God and then trust him, for he is far more powerful than any enemy we face on earth.

PSALM 57

Be exalted, O God, above the highest heavens!
May your glory shine over all the earth.

– Psalm 57:5

My name is mercy. Come and take refuge in the shadow of my wings. Nestle in close until the storms pass by. Though life feels out of control, I am fulfilling my purpose for you. I am saving you and showing you my steadfast love and faithfulness, even through this trial.

When the beasts attack and people come at you with words that pierce your heart like arrows, that is the moment to praise me. Look up—I am exalted in the heavens, and my glory is over all the earth! Don't focus on the things that weigh down your soul. Anchor your heart in me and you will not be moved by the storms of life.

Praise me with melody and music. Wake the dawn with your worship. Sing among the nations. For though your troubles are many, my steadfast love reaches to the heavens and my faithfulness to the clouds. I will be glorified in the earth and in your life.

Whatever our problems may be, God is greater. We can praise him even before he has brought resolution to our difficulties because we know he is faithful and loving, and his glory will prevail.

PSALM 58

The godly will rejoice when they see injustice avenged.

— Psalm 58:10

I am the righteous judge and the true King. My decrees and judgments are right, and my words are true. Others speak lies with venom in their hearts, but I speak words of life and light and love.

Incline your heart to listen to me. Spend time with me so you can recognize my still, small voice. My sheep know my voice and follow me. The closer you stay to me, the more you will hear.

Those who don't follow me will hear me differently. They will tell you I'm silent. Or they will hear truth and become angry, and rightly so because they will one day be judged by my righteous decrees. Pay no attention to them—just keep following me. Rest in my justice, for it is life and joy to those who follow me.

The words of this psalm can be shocking to our modern ears, particularly when we think of it being sung in church, as the title indicates. But when we are faced with injustice, we are rightly angered. It is comforting to remember that God is just, and he will judge evil.

PSALM 59

Each morning I will sing with joy about your unfailing love.
For you have been my refuge, a place of safety when I am in distress.

– Psalm 59:16

You get caught up in your troubles. You gaze at the problems and obstacles you face and feel overwhelmed and in despair. Turn to me. Fix your eyes on me. I am here, ready to meet you and help you overcome the challenges of life. I see the problems that worry you so much, but I am infinitely greater than all those things. Gaze at me, focusing on my steadfast love and almighty power, and everything else will fade into the background.

When the time is right, I will make everything good again. I will judge evil and restore my people to glory. I am preparing a new heaven and a new earth, and soon I will return and make all things right.

But for now, trust me to be your strength and fortress. Sing to me, your refuge in the day of distress. I love you with a steadfast love. I see you, I meet you, and I rouse myself to help you.

When we feel threatened, we want the problem to be fixed. We want God to act on our timetable—now. But it is good for us to wait patiently for God's timing, and to trust that he does all things well.

PSALM 60

Please help us against our enemies, for all human help is useless.
With God's help we will do mighty things, for he will trample down our foes.

– Psalm 60:11-12

I discipline you in love. The hard things that feel like punishments are invitations for you to return to me. They are to help you grow and learn to trust me. When the task or trial before you seems too difficult, remember that you are mine, and everything I have called you to, I will enable you to accomplish.

See, I have set up a banner. It says "The Lord's People." Run to it and be safe. Come to me, the only one who can save you. The help of humans is vain, but with my help you can do anything I ask you to do.

The whole earth is mine! I set up rulers and kingdoms and take them down again to serve my eternal purpose of saving people for myself. I speak and act with holiness and justice. I will triumph over all my enemies, bringing justice to the earth. Indeed, I have already conquered sin and death. So come to me when everything seems wrong and you will see that I am making everything right.

In our battles against the world, the flesh, and the devil, we must remember that our strength lies in our reliance on God. The more we trust him rather than our own flesh, the more we will experience victory over sin.

PSALM 61

From the ends of the earth, I cry to you for help when my
heart is overwhelmed. Lead me to the towering rock of safety.

– Psalm 61:2

I hear every cry. You feel like I am far away, as though you are calling to me from the ends of the earth, but I am closer than your next breath, right here beside you. Lean on me when your heart is faint. I am your refuge, a strong tower to keep you safe from harm.

Come, dwell with me. I am your abiding place. Take refuge under my wings, for there you will find a safe and secure resting place. Stay here next to my heart, even when the day rushes in and chaos is all around you. Keep resting in me.

I am the true King, enthroned forever in heaven. Yet you have a place in my courts. A home and a crown awaits you there. And Jesus daily pleads for you before my throne. You are my dear child, redeemed and forever in my care. Rest in that truth. Feel the security of knowing that you belong to me and my steadfast love rests on you.

Each day we can take shelter under God, who is our towering rock of safety. Today, imagine yourself nestled in close to him, like a baby bird snuggled under its mother's wing, safe from the storm.

PSALM 62

Let all that I am wait quietly before God, for my hope is in him.

– Psalm 62:5

When everyone is against you, when they hurl words like battering rams against your soul—wait on me. Sit silently before me and wait for your salvation. I am your rock and your fortress. When everything around you is shaking, your foundation in me is steadfast.

True hope, certain salvation, is found only in me. Trust me at all times, when things are well and you are tempted to trust in your own strength and on hard days when you have nowhere else to turn. Pour out your heart to me and rest in my strength. Hoping in anything other than me will lead to disappointment, but if you hope in me, you will never be disappointed. I keep all my promises, and I have promised to save you and to love you forever.

All power belongs to me, and I love you with a steadfast love. Find safety in my strong arms. Trust, hope, wait. I will save you.

I love how the verse above acknowledges that sometimes—perhaps most of the time—it takes all of our effort and strength to wait on God. Today, make a conscious decision to look to him and his unfailing love and ignore the difficulties all around you. Choose trust rather than worry.

PSALM 63

O God, you are my God; I earnestly search for you.
My soul thirsts for you; my whole body longs for you
in this parched and weary land where there is no water.

– P s a l m 6 3 : 1

Insatiable thirst. Parched soul. Fainting faith. I see where you are; I know how desperate you feel. In these moments of pain, come to my sanctuary. Gaze on me—behold my power and glory in my Word and in the world I have made.

My steadfast love is better than life. I satisfy your soul, so that you leave my presence feeling as though you've just had a delectable feast. When you come to me with your emptiness, I fill you with good things. Your cup overflows with blessing when you come to me in humble expectancy.

Think of me when you toss and turn through the night. In the darkness, meditate on my loving, faithful care—not on your problems. The shadows you see are my wings of love, bending low to encircle you and hold you close. Cling to me and I will hold you up.

If you are not desperately longing for God as David was when he wrote these words, make this psalm your prayer. Ask God to give you that kind of longing for him. Lift your hands and ask him to fill you with good things.

March
11

PSALM 64

The godly will rejoice in the LORD and find shelter in him.
And those who do what is right will praise him.

– Psalm 64:10

I hear your voice. Just as you know my voice, I know yours because you are my beloved child. I listen to your complaints. Even when you speak without knowledge and doubt me, I hear every word and patiently answer you.

Hear my answer: I will preserve you in the face of the thing you dread most. I will hide you from secret dangers. People and problems take aim against you and lie in wait to ambush you, but I will save you. I bring wicked schemers to nothing. They may plan for your harm, but I plan for your good—and my plans always prevail in the end.

So place your trust in me, the one who can help you. Ponder all I have done for you. Think of my faithfulness to previous generations, how I save those who take refuge in me. Rejoice in my goodness and justice. Take heart, for I am working my purposes throughout the earth and in your life.

We long for the day when God will conquer evil and make everything right. Pray for God to act in such a way that everyone will proclaim his mighty acts and realize the amazing things he has done.

PSALM 65

Though we are overwhelmed by our sins, you forgive them all.

– Psalm 65:3

Here is what I do for you: I hear your prayers. I forgive your sins. I bring you near, inviting you to draw in close and dwell with me. I satisfy you with good things. I am your hope, to the ends of the earth and the farthest seas. I still the roaring waves and tumbling mountains and thronging crowds.

I visit the earth and water it, bringing forth a rich harvest. I provide grain and make it grow. I crown the year with bounty so that even the hardened tire tracks overflow with abundance. You will be so blessed that the footprints you leave behind will become a source of life and blessing to others.

The whole earth sings with joy over my works. Look at the meadows clothed in flowers and dotted with dew—decked out to welcome the morning. Join their anthem of joy, singing with awe over all the good blessings I shower down on you.

This psalm of praise gives us a long list of things to be thankful for and plenty of reasons to praise God. Let these words lift your heart in gratitude and help you trust God more as you see his power in nature.

March
13

PSALM 66

Come and listen, all you who fear God,
and I will tell you what he did for me.

– Psalm 66:16

The earth shouts my name. It reflects my glory. Everything I've made says, "How awesome is God!"

Come, see what I have done. When I brought my people out of slavery in Egypt, I let my people pass through the waters on dry ground while their enemies drowned. Throughout the generations, I have kept the nations in check, intervening when evil grew too great. I have kept your soul secure and given you a firm place to stand. I have brought you through the fires of testing and freed you from the floodwaters that threatened you.

Pull up a chair and sit in my presence. Draw near and tell me your struggles and your joys. I love you with a steadfast love, and I delight to be with you. Indeed, all these things I have done so that you could draw near to me and call me your Father. Walk in the garden with me and let us talk as dear friends.

When was the last time you told someone else about how good God has been to you? Seek an opportunity to publicly praise him today.

March 14

PSALM 67

May the nations praise you, O God. Yes, may all the nations praise you.

– Psalm 67:5

Grace and blessing—these are the things I love to pour out on my people. Hold up your hands and receive my gifts. Watch my love overflow and run down your arms like water from a waterfall.

Lift up your face so that you can see my smile. I shine down on you with my gracious favor, and others can see me in you. Do you long for your loved ones to know me? Then gaze on me. Spend time with me in the Bible and in prayer. My glory and goodness will be written all over your face, and people will see who I am because of you.

Lead all the nations to praise me and sing for joy at all I have done. I have judged the people with equity and blessed the earth with bounty. My power is visible in everything I have made, and my gracious blessing rests on my people.

These verses are a rallying cry for world missions. May we continue to spread the gospel until the whole world praises the Lord! What can you do today to support mission work around the world?

PSALM 68

Let the godly rejoice. Let them be glad in
God's presence. Let them be filled with joy.

– Psalm 68:3

I am on the move. I rise up and my enemies scatter. I ride through the deserts and go before you when you march through the wilderness. I lead the triumphal procession of my redeemed people. And after I myself was the final sacrifice, I ascended on high, where I now rule with righteousness and justice. I do big things, things that cause the world to stand in awe of my power.

But I am also God who dwells with you. Born impoverished in a stable, on the run as a refugee, and living the life of a nomad—all to draw you to myself. I am father to the fatherless, protector of widows, the one who sets the lonely in families and leads prisoners into prosperity.

I draw near in love and lavish you with the gift of my presence. I am bearing you up, even this moment. You are safe in my arms. Do you trust my great love for you?

Let these words cause your heart to swell with praise to the One who rules over the earth but also cares enough to be a father to the fatherless and a defender of widows. God uses his immense power to care for us, even down to the tiny details of our lives.

PSALM 69

The humble will see their God at work and be glad.
Let all who seek God's help be encouraged.

– Psalm 69:32

You feel as if you are drowning. Life is threatening to take over, and you can barely keep your head above water. You can't get your footing, and the floodwaters are rushing in. You've asked me for help, but nothing seems to be happening. Your voice is hoarse with crying, and your eyes are fatigued from watching for me.

Take heart. I have been there. I know what you are going through. I went through all the same things you do—and even worse—for you. I understand. At the right time, and not a minute before, I will answer.

My abundant and steadfast love is forever. I will snatch you from the rushing waves and set your feet on a firm rock. I will give you a song to sing. I am the rock of ages—trust me. My salvation is more than enough to save you from the floodwaters rushing in today and the fires of eternal hell. Everyone who trusts in me will rejoice in my deliverance.

Do you feel as if the floodwaters are up to your neck and you are about to drown? Tell God about it, and then praise him that he hears the cries of the needy.

PSALM 70

May all who search for you be filled with joy and gladness in you.
May those who love your salvation repeatedly shout, "God is great!"

– P s a l m   7 0 : 4

People are always in a rush, hurrying to and fro in their activities while they anxiously watch time pass by. When you're in trouble you want me to fix it immediately. If my deliverance doesn't come on your timetable, you think I'm not listening or don't care about your problems. And if everything is going well, you beg me to slow time down.

I am never in a hurry. I am the eternal God. I see the end from the beginning, and I do everything at the right time—not a moment sooner, and never too late. My deliverance comes at just the right time to rescue you and bring glory to my name.

Rest in my eternal goodness. Cease from your anxious rushing, slow down your soul, and trust me. Stop trying to hurry my perfect will.

There is often an urgency to our prayers, but as we sit in God's presence, his gentle voice reminds us to be patient. He is in control, and we can trust that he will do all things well.

PSALM 71

Now that I am old and gray, do not abandon me, O God.
Let me proclaim your power to this new generation,
your mighty miracles to all who come after me.

– Psalm 71:18

Refuge. Rock. Fortress. Hope. This is what I am for you. A rescuer and deliverer. The one you can trust. I will never forsake you. Before you were conceived, I saw you. In your childhood I rescued you, keeping you safe and guiding your ways. In your old age, I will still be your safe place, the one who keeps you in the palm of my hand.

I am your continual hope. My righteous acts and deeds of salvation are beyond counting. Now it is time for you to declare my goodness to the next generation. Tell them about the way I saved you. Describe my power. Show them how my righteousness reaches to the heavens. Make sure they hear about my faithfulness throughout your whole life. In your words and your actions, pass on praise and joy. This is your lifelong task, your purpose even in old age. For I am with you always, rescuing you and giving you reason to hope until the day I bring you to glory.

This psalm reminds us of God's faithfulness throughout our days, from childhood to old age. As you think back on your life so far and look forward to the time you have left, thank God for the ways he has cared for you and ask him to continue to use you for his glory.

March
19

PSALM 72

Praise the LORD God, the God of Israel, who alone does
such wonderful things. Praise his glorious name forever!
Let the whole earth be filled with his glory.

– Psalm 72:18-19

This is the kind of King I am: just and righteous. Defender of the poor. Deliverer of the oppressed. Punisher of the oppressor. As long as the sun rises, throughout all generations, I will pour down goodness and blessing like rain on my people. My name and my Kingdom will endure forever in righteousness.

Won't you let me rule your life and your heart? I am the only true King, the final authority over all things. One way or another, you will submit to my will—either by choice or by chance. So choose me. Pursue justice and righteousness, peace and blessing.

You are my royal heir. I have promised you an inheritance with Christ. Start now to pursue my Kingdom agenda. Fight for the oppressed, serve the poor, and bring righteousness and justice everywhere you go. Serve my people, my earth. And look forward to the day when you will enter into my throne room and hear me say, "Well done! Enter into my rest."

This psalm honors David's rule and looks forward to the righteous reign of Christ at the end of days. As you read these words, pray these things would be true of your earthly leaders and thank God that they will be perfectly fulfilled when Jesus returns.

PSALM 73

*As for me, how good it is to be near God! I have made the Sovereign
LORD my shelter, and I will tell everyone about the wonderful things you do.*

– Psalm 73:28

Sometimes it seems to you like the wrong people prosper. People who are arrogant and unscrupulous succeed. They get the promotions and the fancy houses, while godly people putter along in obscurity. You wonder if I'm blessing the wrong people.

Don't worry—in the end, those who love and trust me will receive an eternal reward, while the proud and malicious who have not trusted me will suffer the eternal fires of hell. I am just and righteous, and all my judgments are good and right.

Do you want to see my perspective on this? Do you want to glimpse what is really going on beneath the surface? Go to church. Worship and learn with other believers. Dig into the truth of my Word. As you worship and learn together, you can draw near to me and find true treasure. I am the strength of your heart and your portion forever. Because you have me, you have eternal riches that truly satisfy your soul.

It's tempting to be jealous of the people who seem to have it all in this life, especially if they got rich through unethical means. But God gives us the right perspective—true wealth is found in knowing him and having the security of eternal life with him.

PSALM 74

Remember your covenant promises,
for the land is full of darkness and violence!

– P s a l m   7 4 : 2 0

Your nation seems to be struggling. Wickedness is in vogue and evil is tolerated. Sometimes it seems hopeless, as if my very presence has left the earth, or at least your little plot of earth.

But the truth is, I am always at work, bringing salvation to every corner of the globe—even yours. I divided the Red Sea and crushed Israel's enemies. I brought forth water from a rock, proving that I can provide for my people even in the wilderness, even when there are no options left. I display my power in nature and cause the sun to rise each day. I have fixed the boundaries of the earth and the seasons of life. Nothing happens outside my will.

Don't fret over the disasters and dangers in the world. I will not forget the promises I have made to you. I will rescue the poor and needy and arise to defend the defenseless. I will bring you safely through life and carry you to my side. I am still working all my good purposes in your life and on the earth.

Set this psalm beside the daily news and you will be able to pray it with conviction. Things in this life are not as they should be. But we can rest in the knowledge that God is at work, and he has already won the victory over Satan.

March

22

PSALM 75

It is God alone who judges; he decides who will rise and who will fall.

– Psalm 75:7

When the earth shakes, I am the one who steadies it. When the proud boast and the wicked work their evil, I am the one who puts them in their place. I cast down everything that raises itself in defiance against me, but I raise up those who humbly bow before me.

Take heart. At just the right time, I will judge the earth in righteousness. I will utter a word, and everything will be made right. These things do not take place on your timetable, but rest assured, justice is coming. I am at work, and everything I do is good.

For now, rejoice in my righteousness. Take comfort in my justice, humbly resting in my sovereign will and my perfect timing. I am making everything as it should be—just be patient with the process.

These words offer a steadying perspective when we see the evil in the world. We should start out by thanking God for who he is and telling of his wonderful deeds. Then we can trust that he will bring justice to the earth in his perfect timing.

PSALM 76

You stand up to judge those who do evil, O God,
and to rescue the oppressed of the earth.

– Psalm 76:9

My name is known throughout the earth. I am above all rulers and nations. I thwart the schemes of evildoers and bring proud nations down to rubble. No one can stand against my will and prevail.

Even the nations that deny and oppose me will one day acknowledge that I am the Lord, the Almighty, and there is no other. How much more shall you, the one I love, praise me!

Those who stand against me fear what I will do to them, but you stand in awe before me. And you rejoice that my power is in you, too. I dwell in your heart because you trust in me. I give you strength to withstand Satan's temptations and the evil desires within you. I fight your enemies within and without—all you must do is wait and worship.

One day every person who opposes God will be humbled. It is far better to humble ourselves before him now than to wait until he does it for us. Confess your sins to God and purpose in your heart to submit to him and honor him as Lord in every area of your life.

March
24

PSALM 77

I think of God, and I moan, overwhelmed with longing for his help.

– Psalm 77:3

I see your worry and distress. You are in trouble, and you look back on happier times and wonder if life will ever be good again. You beg me to remind you of the songs you used to sing. You ask if I have forgotten you.

I will never forget you. Through your sleepless nights, I am with you. As you toss and turn, remind yourself of all I have done. Meditate on my faithfulness through the ages. Sing songs of praise against the darkness. Who is like me? I am the God who works wonders. I redeemed my people from slavery and your soul from death. Even the mighty seas tremble before me. Storms crash and lightning bolts flash—reminders of my great power. Tornadoes and earthquakes are under my command.

The circumstances of your life are under my command as well. Even when you can't see it, everything that happens to you bears my fingerprint. In my providence, I am making a way for you to pass through this sea of difficulty. I am with you always and will lead you safely home to my side.

Perhaps you identify with these words of desperate longing. Maybe you feel as if God has rejected you. Follow the advice of the psalmist and meditate on God's holiness and power. Remember how he led his people through the sea, and trust that he will do it again in your life.

PSALM 78:1-20

We will tell the next generation about the glorious deeds of the LORD, about his power and his mighty wonders.

– Psalm 78:4

Do you want hope, both for yourself and to pass on to the next generation? Remember everything I have done. Do not forget the example of those who have gone before. This is the key to hope, for the testimony of others will remind you of my faithfulness and cause you to look to me alone for salvation.

I led my people through the desert; I will also lead you through your desert of difficulty. I brought my people through the sea on dry land; I will also bring you through the waters and save you. I gave my people water from a rock; I will also give you refreshment from the most unlikely sources.

Despite all the miracles I did for them, the Israelites rebelled against me. Learn from their example. Receive my salvation with joy and keep following me. I am your only hope in life and in death. Trust in me, for I will take care of you.

The next generation needs to hear of God's greatness from those who have gone before. Don't assume that a child is too young to understand, or spend time only with those who are at your same maturity level. Today, find someone younger—either in age or in spiritual maturity—and tell them about God's greatness.

PSALM 78:21-29

They ate the food of angels! God gave them all they could hold.

– Psalm 78:25

Do you remember what I did right after the people grumbled in the wilderness? I was rightly angered by their sin, but I still sent manna from heaven—the bread of angels. I am gracious and merciful, and I satisfy all the needs of my people, even when they turn their backs on me.

I am the Bread of Heaven. I feed my people with good gifts. I meet your needs in abundance by giving you myself. I satisfy your deep soul hunger. Feed on me in my Word and be filled. Feast on my goodness even in the wilderness.

Do you see how good I have been to you? I will keep doing it. The gates of heaven are cast open wide to pour down manna from heaven.

Receive it with joy!

Jesus said that he is the Bread of Life (John 6:35, 58). He satisfies our deepest hunger and gives us true life. Today, feast on him. Forego the comforts and pleasures that the world uses to temporarily satisfy its soul longings, and instead feed on the true life found in Jesus.

PSALMS 79, 83

Help us, O God of our salvation! Help us for the glory of your name. Save us and forgive our sins for the honor of your name.

– P s a l m 7 9 : 9

Defeat is bitter. Some days life kicks you, and then when you get up, it kicks you again and sits on top of you. Sometimes your plans and accomplishments lie in ruins at your feet. In this life you will experience trouble and distress; you can count on it.

But I will not always keep silent. One day I will make all things right. Those who have done unspeakable evil to my people will be consumed. On that day, everyone will know that I alone am God Most High and will bow before me.

While you wait for me to set right everything that is wrong, trust me. Trust that I will keep my promise to do justly. Trust that I have established a place in heaven just for you, a place I have been preparing throughout the ages. Trust that your troubles, those difficulties that loom so large right now, will seem insignificant and small on that day.

Psalm 79 describes Jerusalem's fall to the Assyrians in 586 BC. Jerusalem lay in ruins. It seemed as though God had abandoned his people. Maybe your life feels like that right now. Let the words of these two psalms be your prayer for justice, and then in faith thank God for his care for you (79:13) and his coming just rule (83:18).

PSALM 80

Turn us again to yourself, O God of Heaven's Armies. Make your face shine down upon us. Only then will we be saved.

– Psalm 80:7

I am your Shepherd. With my rod and staff I turn you back to the right way whenever you veer off the path. I clear space for you to feed on good grass. I provide shade to keep you cool and give you refreshing water in the heat of the day.

Yet you spurn these good gifts. You run after lesser things and try out other gods—chasing money and sex and false religions that seem to require less of you. Those things can never satisfy.

It is not too late. Turn back to me, and I will turn to you. I will restore you for my own name's sake, because you are mine. I will make you strong and give you life. Call upon me, and I will shine my face toward you and give you peace and blessing. I am the only one who can save you.

The repeated refrain "turn us again to yourself" is a prayer we should continually offer to God. The good news is that when we turn to God, he lovingly shines his gracious favor on us.

March

29

PSALM 81

Oh, that my people would listen to me!
Oh, that Israel would follow me, walking in my paths!

– Psalm 81:13

Rise with the dawn and shout a song of praise. I am the God who rescued Moses and raised him up to deliver my people. I freed you from slavery to sin and self. I answered your cries of distress and saved you.

I alone am God, and if you serve me with your whole heart, I will pour out all the covenant blessing of my loving and faithful presence in your life. Open wide your mouth and I will fill it with good things.

Yet so often you don't listen to my gentle voice reminding you of the right path. You stray away and do things that go against my laws. Return to me! Follow my ways. Turn toward me with a tender heart. Then I will feed you with the Bread of Life and satisfy you with honey from the rock—abundant sweetness beneath the hard.

God's entreaty to listen to him and follow him is connected to a promise: If we walk in his paths, he will feed us with the finest wheat and satisfy us with honey from the rock. The sacrifices we make to follow him are small in comparison with the generous blessing we receive in return.

March
30

PSALM 82

Rise up, O God, and judge the earth, for all the nations belong to you.

– P s a l m   8 2 : 8

Are you questioning my judgments? Do you wonder why bad people seem to succeed while good people are afflicted? Do you wish I would deliver my people from difficulty right now? Do you think I should overthrow the leaders who rule without knowledge or understanding, the ones who shake the earth with their disordered judgments?

Never fear, I am good and I am on my throne. I am the very definition of justice, and all my judgments are good and right. I will defend the cause of the destitute and rescue the needy and right every wrong.

These promises will come true, but it will be on my perfect timetable. In mercy I wait for people from every nation to hear about me and be saved. I am giving people time to turn toward me with repentant hearts. The delays and obstacles that you fight so hard against are evidence of my patience, forbearance, and kindness. Rest in my judgments, for they are always right. Wait for my timing, for it is a mercy.

Revelation 11:15 describes voices in heaven shouting, "The world has now become the Kingdom of our Lord and of his Christ, and he will reign forever and ever." One day every knee will bow before Jesus. That is a promise we can cling to when the world seems to be filled with evil and injustice.

PSALM 84

*What joy for those whose strength comes from the LORD, who have
set their minds on a pilgrimage to Jerusalem. When they walk through
the Valley of Weeping, it will become a place of refreshing springs.*

– Psalm 84:5-6

That homesickness you sometimes feel even when you are home—that
bittersweet yearning you sense even on days (or especially on days)
of delight—that is a longing for me. Your flesh and heart cry out for your
true home, heaven, where you will live forever with the lover of your soul.

Come to me and abide in me, and you will find deep, joyful blessing.
When you go through dry and wearying times, you will still find
refreshment in me. The dry ground in your soul will spring up with living
water. You will journey from strength to strength.

A day in my house is better than a thousand anywhere else. I am your
sun and shield, your delight and protection. I crown you with glory and
honor. I withhold no good thing from you, for I do all things for your
benefit. This is the joy of abiding in me and making your pilgrimage
through life all about being near me and coming home to me.

Every longing we have on earth is a shadow longing for the true
satisfaction we can find only in God himself. Turn your desires
over to him, and see how he will refresh you.

April

April
1

PSALM 85

Unfailing love and truth have met together.
Righteousness and peace have kissed!

– Psalm 85:10

See all I do for you: I forgive your iniquity. I cover your sin, even the things you want to hide from everyone. I withhold my anger, even when you deserve my wrath. I restore and revive you and shower you with my steadfast love. I grant you salvation—abundant, everlasting life. And I am near to you, a companion in your suffering.

Listen as I speak, for my words are peace to you. Steadfast love and faithfulness meet in me. Righteousness and peace kiss each other, mingling in perfect harmony at the cross. Faithfulness springs up from the ground and righteousness falls from the sky. Everywhere you turn, you are surrounded by my goodness.

Rest in all these good gifts I've given you. They will carry you through all the things you're facing. You have everything you need in me.

We often pray for revival and wait for a dramatic act of God, but anytime we ponder all that God has done, our souls will be strengthened and revived. In God righteousness and peace mingle in perfect harmony—he is holy, and we are forgiven.

April
2

PSALM 86

*Teach me your ways, O LORD, that I may live according to
your truth! Grant me purity of heart, so that I may honor you.*

– Psalm 86:11

You say you are poor and needy, and indeed you are . . . apart from me. But when you lift your soul to me, acknowledging your desperation and being honest about your situation, then I will answer you. I will pour out my grace on you.

There is no one like me among the gods, no equal to my power and love, no one who does such wondrous deeds. One day everyone will bow before me. They will glorify my name, for I am great and I alone am God.

I have placed my steadfast love on you, and it will never depart from you. I have delivered you from the curse of sin and death. I am merciful and gracious, slow to anger and abounding in steadfast love and faithfulness. I have turned my face to shine my light upon you and give you my strength. You are favored and adored. Rejoice in your eternal, unchangeable identity as my child.

Even as we cry to God for help and deliverance, we need to praise him for his character and commit ourselves to obeying him. When we submit to him, he pours down blessing upon blessing.

3

PSALM 87

O city of God, what glorious things are said of you!

– Psalm 87:3

All who know me are headed home to heaven—my eternal dwelling place and yours. It is a glorious, beautiful place of joy and rest and worship. It is your true home. I can't wait for you to join me!

People from every tribe and tongue and nation will find their home with me. The Jews thought salvation was only for them, but I have made Gentiles my covenant people, recipients of my blessing as well. Anyone whose name is written in the Book of Life has been made my child through the blood of Jesus, and their home is in Zion.

Heaven is your true joy. It is where every longing of your heart will find full satisfaction. Look forward to that day when you will see me face-to-face. Enjoy my blessings now as but a tiny foretaste of the magnificent, indescribable blessings to come.

This psalm paints a glorious picture of Jerusalem, the city of God. But it points to a greater reality—that everyone who trusts in Christ for salvation is given the rights of citizenship in heaven. Live today as a stranger in this world who is looking forward to heaven, the place where you really belong.

April
4

PSALM 88

O LORD, I cry out to you. I will keep on pleading day by day.
– Psalm 88:13

I know that the world is full of suffering. I hear the prayers of those who are at death's door, who have no strength left. They feel as though I have left them, that I have shunned them. The waves of grief lie heavy over them.

But I will not cast off anyone who calls on my name. I hear every cry and groan. I am here, right beside those who suffer. Right beside you, on your days of deep darkness just as on your days of light. Keep crying out to me, keep coming to me for help, for I am your hope and your deliverer.

You can't measure my love for you by how pleasant or painful your life is right now. In the light of eternity, your time of suffering is but a passing shadow, here one moment and gone the next. I am with you in your suffering, loving you and holding you fast. Trust me. Lean into me and feel my embrace.

Though this psalm doesn't offer a lot of hope, we also encounter days when we can't see any reason for hope. If you can identify with the psalmist who wrote these words, pray them and then let God speak his love over you. If you can't identify with these words, pray for people you may know who have no hope and ask God to use you to encourage them today.

PSALM 89

*O LORD God of Heaven's Armies! Where is there anyone
as mighty as you, O LORD? You are entirely faithful.*

– Psalm 89:8

My steadfast love is forever. My faithfulness goes on from generation to generation. My covenant promises—to make you a people for myself, to live with you and be your King and Good Shepherd—these will never fail because they depend on my faithfulness, not yours.

The heavens sing my praises, and the gathering of my people in worship honors my name. Who is like me, the ruler over all? The heavens are mine, and the earth is mine. Who is mighty but me? My throne is founded on righteousness and justice because that is who I am, from eternity past to eternity future.

You are my blessed child. You walk in light even though darkness is all around you. My steadfast love shields you from evil. My power allows you to go from strength to strength. I will establish you and keep you forever because you are dear to me.

God's promises to establish David's throne forever were fulfilled in Jesus. He is our eternal King, the one who guarantees that we will never be rejected or cast away from God's presence.

PSALM 90

Teach us to realize the brevity of life, so that we may grow in wisdom.
– Psalm 90:12

In every generation, from Adam until now, I am a dwelling place for all who come to me. Even from everlasting to everlasting, from before the earth was formed to this moment and forevermore—I am God. Time, which feels to you like a box to entrap you, doesn't even exist for me except as a tool I use to bring people to myself. All that you see, all that worries you today, is like a mist, here for a moment and gone by midmorning.

Let these truths give you perspective. Nothing that worries you today is as big a deal as it seems. True wisdom is trusting me and letting everything in this world get small as you gaze on the beauty of my holiness.

Let me satisfy you with my love—it is all you need. Rejoice and be glad in my steadfast affection. You have been afflicted for many days, and for many years evil has prevailed on the earth, but I will restore that to you. Eternal joy awaits you in heaven. Trust me that it will be worth all the pain, all the waiting.

Life is short, but God is eternal, and he cares for us each day of our lives. Let these words help you gain perspective on the brevity of life so you can enjoy the blessings and endure the trials God places in your life.

April
7

PSALM 91

Those who live in the shelter of the Most High
will find rest in the shadow of the Almighty.

– Psalm 91:1

Live in my shelter, for I will protect you. Abide in my shadow, for I will give you shade. I am your refuge and shelter, the one who delivers you from the snares and dangers in your path. I will cover you with my wings, and you will be safely snuggled close against my heart.

My faithfulness encircles you, so you do not need to fear the terrors of night or the attacks of the day. My promises are your armor and protection. No evil shall befall you; everything that happens is in my good plan for you. People strategize to harm you, but in my plan those things are turned to good, to save many.

Because you hold fast to me in love, I will deliver you. I protect those who know my name, who trust in my character and my promises. When you call, I will answer you. I will be with you in trouble; I will rescue and honor you. I will satisfy you and show you my salvation.

What joy and rest there is in the words of this psalm. Read them slowly, letting them wash over you and comfort you. Then make a list of all God's promises.

April
8

PSALM 92

You thrill me, LORD, with all you have done for me!
I sing for joy because of what you have done.

– Psalm 92:4

This is a song of Sabbath joy. Rest is my gift to you, a declaration of my steadfast love and faithfulness. Let the discipline of Sabbath rest grow your faith as you trust that six days are enough for work, and the seventh is a holy day set apart for rejuvenation and relationship. Make music and sing songs of joy. Meditate on my great works and my tender thoughts toward you. Let my love pour over you, refresh you, and anoint you like fresh oil.

The day you set aside for worship, rest, and fellowship is your key to a flourishing spiritual life. It is your vital connection to the stream of living water. Those who are planted in my house have a rich and full life of the soul. When they are old, they will be more alive than ever, for the years of learning of me will flow out of them in new life. They will bear the fruit of righteousness until the end of their days.

Do you want a deep and full life? Spend each Sabbath in my house, with my people, in rest and worship.

When was the last time you used the Sabbath as it was intended: for rest and worship and fellowship? No striving, no catching up on work—just trusting that if you give this day to God, he will take care of the rest of the week? Add this discipline into your life and see how God uses it.

April
9

PSALM 93

Mightier than the violent raging of the seas, mightier than the breakers on the shore—the LORD above is mightier than these!

– Psalm 93:4

I am King over all the earth. I am robed in majesty and strength. I have created and established the earth, setting the boundaries of the sea and filling the earth with my breath. Everything stands or falls at my command.

So today, if the floods threaten to overwhelm you, if you feel as though you are drowning in sorrow or trouble, remember that I am mightier than all the roaring of the seas. You have nothing to fear because everything is under my control, and at just the right time I will command the wind and waves to be still.

Trust my decrees, for I always do what is right. Even this storm you are facing is in my plan and from my hand. Trust me. Rest in my power and love for you, for I do all things in holiness and righteousness.

If the floodwaters are threatening to drown you, use these words as a victory cry. God is bigger, he is stronger, and he is on his throne. You can trust that he will take care of everything that concerns you.

PSALM 94

I cried out, "I am slipping!" but your unfailing love, O LORD, supported me.
When doubts filled my mind, your comfort gave me renewed hope and cheer.

– P s a l m   9 4 : 1 8 - 1 9

Today it seems like the world is spiraling out of control. The wicked seem to be winning. You cry out to me to work justice. Don't fear—I made the ear, so surely I can be trusted to hear your cries for help. I formed the eye, so surely you can trust me to see what's going on. I created knowledge, so surely I know all things, even the thoughts of every person.

These troubles that surround you are all under my control. I use them to help you grow, and then at the right time I take them away and give you rest. I will never forsake you or abandon you. I will work justice in all things.

Though people may seek to harm you, your foot will not slip, for I am your helper. You do not suffer alone, for I am your consolation to cheer you. Though the world rises against you, I am your stronghold and the rock of your refuge.

When doubts fill your mind, let God comfort you with the truth of his Word and give you renewed hope and cheer. He is your mighty rock, and he will bring justice to the earth.

PSALM 95

*Come, let us worship and bow down. Let us kneel before
the LORD our maker, for he is our God. We are the
people he watches over, the flock under his care.*

– Psalm 95:6-7

Sing with joy at my presence. Let praise and thanksgiving be ever on your lips, for I am the great King above all gods. I hold the depths of the earth in my hands. The mighty mountains are mine, and the roaring sea, for I made them all out of nothing.

I am your maker, but I am also your God. I care for you as a shepherd cares for his sheep, tenderly and gently. You are mine and I am yours.

So don't harden your heart against me. Don't grumble and put me to the test. Don't doubt my goodness, my love, or my power. The proof of my care is all around you. I have rescued you from sin and shown love to you. Soften your heart toward me so I can show you my faithfulness. Come, enter the soul rest that comes from trusting your Good Shepherd to take care of you.

When we consider the greatness of our God, and then consider how tenderly he cares for every detail of our lives, it should cause us to have soft hearts toward him.

PSALM 96

Worship the LORD in all his holy splendor.
Let all the earth tremble before him.

– Psalm 96:9

As you open your eyes to greet the dawn, sing a new song. Forget yesterday's troubles; today's blessings are fresh and new. Praise me for what I am doing now and look with hopeful joy to what I will do in the future.

This day, declare my glory to everyone you meet. Show them my greatness, my splendor and majesty. Tell about my love and power. Remind them of all my marvelous works. Worship me in all my holy magnificence, approaching me with the awe I deserve, for I have power over this life and the next. Say to the nations, "God reigns!" Tell them that I am bringing redemption to the world.

Even the seas and fields rejoice, and the trees sing for joy, for they know that the true King is returning, and with me will come perfect faithfulness and righteousness. When I return, everything will be put right and everyone will live in peace. Won't you join the song of the ages and praise me for this future hope?

In what ways can you worship the Lord today? Here are some ideas: Sing songs of praise. Tell others about his great love. Bring justice and truth to someone who needs help. Or simply spend time with him as you look at nature.

PSALM 97

*The L*ORD *is king! Let the earth rejoice! Let the farthest coastlands be glad.*

– P s a l m   9 7 : 1

Rejoice, for I reign as the only true King over all the earth. Coastlands, clouds, thick darkness—these are merely the foundation of my throne. I shine forth the light of my holiness and the earth trembles. Mountains melt like wax before my power. All of creation acknowledges my sovereignty.

Some people try to deny my power, but one day every knee will bow before me. All the idols people worship instead of me will come to nothing. So worship me now. Take joy in my righteousness. Rest in the knowledge that you are worshiping the true King, the one with all power whose victory is assured.

Consider how I protect and preserve my people. I deliver them from the power of the evil one and cause them to live in joy and light. Come, rejoice in the victory and hope of my holy name.

The day when Jesus returns to reign over the new heaven and new earth will be a day of great joy for those who love him, and terror for those who do not. If you don't anticipate it with joy, examine your heart to see why that is.

PSALM 98

Sing a new song to the LORD, for he has done wonderful deeds. His right hand has won a mighty victory; his holy arm has shown his saving power!

– Psalm 98:1

Sing a new song! I have done marvelous things for you, and each day brings new expressions of my love for you. My right hand and mighty power have rescued you from the curse of sin. I have shown you steadfast love and faithfulness. And not just you, this great salvation is for all people—even the very worst sinner.

Isn't that reason enough to sing and make glorious music to me? This is good news—salvation has come! The true King rules with righteousness and justice, and he is coming back soon to restore all things.

If you can't muster up a song of your own today, join in creation's song. The seas, the rivers, the hills—all of it is praising me. Let them be your voice and allow them to teach you their song of praise to me, the eternal King.

This day, with all its troubles and joys, is the day to begin what you will spend all of eternity doing: praising the eternal King who reigns in victory and justice.

PSALM 99

*Exalt the LORD our God, and worship at his holy
mountain in Jerusalem, for the LORD our God is holy!*

– Psalm 99:9

People tremble before me, and well they should—I am the King. My throne is on angels' wings and the earth shakes before my power. I am holy. I deserve the praise of all people.

Yet I am also near. When you worship, you are coming to my throne. When you call, I answer. I speak to your heart and tell you everything you need to know to follow me this day. I forgive you, no matter how deep your sin or how unworthy you feel. And I will deal justly with everything that concerns you.

Come, pull up a stool near my feet so we can talk. Enter my holy presence with boldness, for you are my dear child. Tell me everything on your heart, for I will answer you.

It is right to approach God with healthy fear. He is holy, and we are not. That is why it is so remarkable that the writer of Hebrews urges us to "come boldly to the throne of our gracious God. There we will receive his mercy" (Hebrews 4:16). Take advantage of the privilege of boldly entering God's throne room as his beloved child today.

April
16

PSALM 100

Enter his gates with thanksgiving; go into his courts
with praise. Give thanks to him and praise his name.

– Psalm 100:4

Let your soul bubble over with gladness. Sing, shout, and speak words of gratitude as you enter my presence. Even the trees and animals make joyful noises—how much more should you! Therefore, let glad thankfulness characterize everything you say and do.

For you know that I am God. I made you, and you are mine. You are my treasure, the sheep of my pasture. You are known and cherished and sought after.

Give thanks and bless my name, for I am good and I bless you with good things. My steadfast love for you endures forever. My faithfulness to you will never end; even your children's children will see my goodness and enjoy my blessing.

God's faithfulness is not just for us; it came down through the generations before us, and it continues for our children and our children's children. Praise God that throughout all ages, his love has never failed and will never fail.

PSALM 101

I will be careful to live a blameless life . . .
I will lead a life of integrity in my own home.

– P s a l m   1 0 1 : 2

Here is the way to live well and leave behind a lasting legacy of faith: Sing of my steadfast love and justice, making music in your heart and with your life. Let truth inform everything you do. Ponder what is right and holy. Walk with integrity, even in your own home where no one can see you. Don't even put worthless idols in front of you. Stay away from perversity as you choose friends and entertainment. Speak the truth in humility and work for justice.

If you do these things, you will be honored for living well. People will remember you with joy and learn from your example. Be one of the faithful in the land—doing right is always worth it.

Using this psalm as inspiration, make your own list of personal commitments or resolutions that will help you live as God has called you to live. What things do you need to do or avoid doing to better obey God and live for him?

PSALM 102

The children of your people will live in security.
Their children's children will thrive in your presence.

– Psalm 102:28

Your cries reach my heart. You feel withered and dried out, lifeless and in despair. Tears fall from your eyes and mingle with your drink. You are lost and alone, wandering through the wilderness.

Look up! I am on my throne. My face is turned toward you, and I listen to your prayers. My ear is inclined to you, and my answer is coming. At the appointed time—and not a moment sooner—I will rise up. Nations will fear me on that day. I will appear in all my glory, and every knee will bow before me. I will free the prisoners so they can declare my greatness. People from every kingdom will worship me.

This is where your hope lies. I laid the foundations of the earth, and even when everything else passes away, I will remain. I stay the same, and my years have no end. Therefore you can dwell securely. You are mine eternally, and nothing can snatch you out of my hand.

The writer of this psalm was in a desperate state. Maybe you can't relate to that experience, but you can imitate the honesty of this prayer. Be honest with God about your struggles, and then rejoice that he laid the foundations of the earth and will be faithful to his promises.

PSALM 103:1-14

*Let all that I am praise the LORD; may I
never forget the good things he does for me.*

– Psalm 103:2

Rouse your soul—every part of you—to bless my name. Such praise will naturally flow from your lips if you think of everything I do for you . . .

I forgive all your sin. I heal all your diseases. I redeem your life from the pit. I crown you with steadfast love and mercy. I satisfy you with good. I renew your youth like the eagle's.

I work righteousness and justice for the oppressed—just think of what I did for Moses and the people of Israel! I am merciful and gracious, slow to anger and abounding in steadfast love. I do not deal with people according to their sins or repay you for your iniquities. My love for you is so great that I cast your sins as far as the east is from the west. I am mindful of your weaknesses, for I have the heart of a compassionate father toward you.

This litany of God's gracious acts ends with the crown jewel: He is a tender and compassionate father to us, bearing with our weakness. If you are struggling with guilt, let these words give you hope and courage. God loves you, he forgives you, and he tenderly cares for all your weaknesses.

PSALM 103:15-22

Our days on earth are like grass; like wildflowers, we bloom and die . . .
But the love of the LORD remains forever with those who fear him.

– P s a l m   1 0 3 : 1 5 ,   1 7

The days of each person's life are brief. You grow up and flourish like a flower, beautiful and fruitful for a time, then the wind passes over and you are gone. Your days on earth are few when compared to eternity. Viewing your life from this perspective helps you not take yourself too seriously.

But my love for you is forever, steadfast from everlasting to everlasting. Your great-great-grandchildren and generations beyond will enjoy my blessing. I will show them my righteousness and faithfulness, just as I have done for you.

My throne is in the heavens, and my rule extends over all. The angels bless me and do my bidding, serving as ministers in my courts and in the world. Everything seen and unseen is in my dominion. So worship and praise me for my great power. Rejoice in my love and serve me with gladness all the days of your brief life.

The frailty of human existence is sometimes cause for great pain, especially when we lose someone we love too soon, but it is also a mercy. God's love is forever, and when we see how brief life is, it helps us see how great his love is in comparison. His love, and our life with him, lasts forever.

PSALM 104

*O Lord, what a variety of things you have made! In wisdom
you have made them all. The earth is full of your creatures.*

– Psalm 104:24

Look at the beautiful world I have created and let it draw your heart to
worship. Light is my garment. The heavens are my tent. The clouds
are my chariot, and I ride the wind. I set the earth on its foundations
and caused the wind to create its depths. Mountains rose and fell to their
appointed places at my word.

I make the springs gush forth to water the earth and satisfy the animals.
The moon marks the seasons and the sun rises and sets according to my
will. Everything happens in its appointed time. I open my hand, and all
the earth is satisfied with the goodness of my provision.

All of this mighty power is on display to remind you that I am the
eternal Creator. Surely if I created and sustain all the natural world, I can
also care for you. Trust in my goodness and love for you. Watch in hope
as I provide everything you need.

The beautiful imagery of this poem of praise causes our hearts
to swell with worship. But notice also how intricate God's care
is. Whatever your worries are today, you can entrust them to the
God who cares even for the birds and mountain goats.

PSALM 105

All this happened so they would follow his decrees and obey his instructions.

– Psalm 105:45

Do you need strength today? Do you wish to feel my presence? Remember all my faithful deeds. Meditate on them and let them remind you of my love. I will never forget you or go back on my promises to you. Even to a thousand generations, I am faithful in my love.

Think of Abraham, Isaac, and Jacob. Ponder the way I cared for them. Consider Joseph and how I preserved his life even when all hope seemed lost. Meditate on Moses and the miraculous way I rescued my people from slavery and led them through the desert. Through all these generations I was keeping my promise to give them an inheritance and be their King.

Now my covenant love rests on you. I will lead you out with joyful songs. I am your King and Shepherd all the days of your life. That is where your strength lies. Trust and believe that I am saving and keeping you this day and always, and let that truth give you strength and hope for everything you face today.

This brief history of God's faithfulness to Israel had a single purpose: to call God's people to obedience. As you rejoice in God's faithful, covenant love, renew your determination to follow him and submit to his will.

PSALM 106

Who can list the glorious miracles of the LORD?
Who can ever praise him enough?

– Psalm 106:2

If you tried to count my mighty deeds, you couldn't do it—there are just too many! And yet you forget my faithfulness. This chronic forgetting of all I have done dates back to Egypt, when my people rebelled and grumbled because they didn't trust me.

Even so, I saved them—for my own sake. I redeemed them from their enemies and led them through the desert. Over and over they doubted my goodness, yet I never abandoned them. Even when they served other gods, I did not stop being good to them and showing them my love. When they cried out to me, I heard them. I remembered my covenant and poured out my steadfast love on them.

And that is how I love you. Even when you grumble and rebel and chase other gods—I still love you with a never-ending love. When you are faithless, I am faithful. Rest in my great love for you. Trust my goodness. I love you from everlasting to everlasting.

This catalog of God's goodness is more than an interesting history lesson. It should be a reminder of God's love for us and a call to learn from others' mistakes. Meditate on God's miracles, praise him for his glorious greatness, and purpose to follow him all your days.

PSALM 107

He satisfies the thirsty and fills the hungry with good things.

– Psalm 107:9

Remember how good I have been to you. When you wandered in the desert, hungry and fainting, you cried out and I led you to a good place. I satisfied the longings of your soul and filled you with good things.

When you sat in darkness and death, when you rejected me over and over again until you came to the end of yourself and cried out to me, I brought you out of darkness into light. I shattered the walls of your prison of guilt and shame and gave you freedom.

When you were a foolish sinner, wallowing in the debris of your bad choices, you cried out to me and I rescued you and healed you with a word. When you chased after wealth and forgot me, I showed you my power in the windstorm and then stilled the raging waves and reminded you of my love.

Let me do it for you again. Let me turn the dry places in your soul into springs of water. Let me raise you up from your affliction and multiply my blessings in your life. Remember my goodness and trust me to do it again.

The things God did for Israel are the same things he does for us—saving, rescuing, and blessing. Thank him today for all the ways he satisfies you and fills you with good things.

PSALM 108

Please help us against our enemies, for all human help is useless.
With God's help we will do mighty things, for he will trample down our foes.

– Psalm 108:12-13

Things may seem hopeless right now, as you look at the battle before you and the tasks yet undone. You wonder if I have left you to struggle through this alone. But I see the end from the beginning. Praise me even in your fears as an expression of faith that I will keep my promises. Anchor your hope in my promises and give thanks for my steadfast love and faithfulness even when you're not sure you believe that I still love you.

My promises are forever. I have promised justice and goodness, and you can be confident that I will follow through. Don't trust what you see now, or the promises other people make. Put your trust in me, for I am the one who saves. What I say is true—you can count on it.

The secret to winning our battles against the world, the flesh, and the devil is to let God fight for us. The help of humans—including ourselves—is worthless. But with God we can do mighty things if we place our confidence in him.

April
26

PSALM 109

*I will give repeated thanks to the L*ORD*, praising him to everyone. For he stands beside the needy, ready to save them from those who condemn them.*

– Psalm 109:30-31

I see it too: This world is full of evil and darkness. I know that from your perspective it seems as though evil has the upper hand. It looks like I'm standing by while innocent people suffer. And so you beg me not to be silent, to stand up for righteousness.

I am not deaf or silent. I see what is going on. More than that, I see the end of the battle. I won at the Cross and I will win at the end of time. Evil has been defeated. So don't fret; don't let the evil that surrounds you cause you to lose hope.

Look instead on my steadfast love. Gaze on the cross and the empty tomb and take courage. Await my deliverance in triumphant hope. My power is greater than the power of evil, and my victory is sure.

This psalm is perhaps the strongest indictment on evil in all of Scripture. In this case David is innocent. He even loves these enemies (verses 4-5), although these are enemies of God himself, truly evil and wicked men. We will probably never be in a position to pray these words for ourselves, but we can pray for an end to evil and for God to care for the needy.

PSALM 110

*The L*ORD *said to my Lord, "Sit in the place of honor at my right hand until I humble your enemies, making them a footstool under your feet."*

– P s a l m   1 1 0 : 1

The battle has been won. I am Jesus your King. The mighty scepter is in my hand, and I rule over my enemies in perfect holiness and justice. Satan has already been defeated; the final outcome is assured.

I am the perfect Lamb and the great High Priest, the one who enables you to stand before the Father, completely forgiven and whole. I am the judge who will return to bring peace and rule in righteousness.

Rejoice that the outcome of the cosmic battle between good and evil is sure. No matter what happens today, I am on my throne. Worship with gladness because I am the victorious King. In the end, that is all that matters.

This messianic psalm affirms God's covenant and assures the hope of future victory. Jesus is our High Priest, interceding on our behalf before God the Father, and he will return to bring justice to the earth.

PSALM 111

How amazing are the deeds of the LORD!
All who delight in him should ponder them.

– Psalm 111:2

Do you need a reason to praise me today? Study my works and be filled with delight. You'll see that everything I do displays my splendor and majesty. Everything I do is righteous. Remember my grace and mercy in saving you, and give thanks.

Do you see my provision for you—how you have everything you need each day? That is evidence of my covenant love. See how my word is trustworthy, how the works of my hands are faithful and just, and thank me for all I have done.

Don't say you can't think of anything to be thankful for. Open your eyes, lift your gaze from your own problems, and you will see me at work all around you. If I have done all of this, then surely you can also trust me to do good things for you today. You can count on me to show you love and to display my power in your life.

Begin today to practice the discipline of gratitude. Each day look for at least three things you can thank God for, and keep a record of them in your journal. As you practice gratitude you will find that your heart changes and you see more of God's goodness.

PSALM 112

How joyful are those who fear the LORD
and delight in obeying his commands.

– Psalm 112:1

Do you know what happens in the life of a person who delights in my Word? Their descendants are mighty in the land. Indeed, entire generations are blessed through them. They have all they need, and they are generous with what they have because they know it comes from my hand. People speak well of them, for they are gracious and merciful toward others. When they die, people remember them with joy.

Best of all, those who fear me and delight in my commandments do not fear bad news. They know I will take care of them, so they are not afraid of anything. In the day of trouble they are not shaken, for I am the anchor of their soul.

These are great benefits—and all come from loving my Word. Won't you open it today, study it, and meditate on it? See how it transforms your life!

Of all the benefits of fearing the Lord and delighting in obeying his commands, the most compelling is that it will cause us not to fear bad news (verse 7). The more you obey God, the more you grow to trust him, and that gives you courage to face any difficulty with hope.

April
30

PSALM 113

*Who can be compared with the LORD our God, who is
enthroned on high? He stoops to look down on heaven and on earth.*

– Psalm 113:5-6

My name—the sum total of who I am—is praised forever, from the rising of the sun to its setting into eternity. There is none like me, high above the nations and glorious in the heavens.

Yet I look down on the people I have made and am moved with compassion. I see the forgotten people who sit in the dust. I see the empty person who has lost everything. I see the one who is sad and barren and alone. I see you in your darkest moments.

I am the God of reversals. I raise up the lowly to a place of honor. The one who had nothing gets all in me. The barren woman receives a house filled with the shouts of happy children. This is who I am, and I will do it for you. So bring me your broken, empty places and let me fill them. Lay bare your losses and sorrows, and I will give you my overflowing, abundant, never-ending blessing.

God's glory is higher than the heavens, but he stoops down to care for those who are needy and destitute. In what ways can you imitate God's care for "the least of these" today?

PSALM 115

*The L*ORD *remembers us and will bless us.*

– Psalm 115:12

Other people chase after idols, after things made by human hands. They worship things that have no life and give no life, and in the end, they become like what they have bowed down their souls to.

But you have placed your trust in me, your Creator and Redeemer. I am your help and shield. I have remembered you—remembered your needs and your weaknesses, remembered my great love for you, remembered my promises—and I will bless you.

As you trust in me, I will multiply your influence and reach. I will bless you with children. I will give you of the bounty of the earth and open wide the spiritual storehouses of heaven.

What a comfort it is that God remembers us. He sees us, he knows our struggles, and he remembers his promises to us. These are things only a living, all-powerful, and all-knowing God can do. Worship him today for his care for you.

May
2

PSALM 116

Let my soul be at rest again, for the LORD has been good to me.
He has saved me from death, my eyes from tears, my feet from stumbling.

– Psalm 116:7-8

Call on me every day, many times a day, in moments of joy and times of sorrow. I incline my ear to you and listen. I hear and I care. When you come into my presence, you will find rest for your soul. There you will be reminded that I deal bountifully with you.

Think of all I have done for you: I have delivered your soul from death, your eyes from tears, and your feet from stumbling. I have lavished blessing after blessing upon you. Even physical death has been transformed from something to be feared into a glorious entrance into your eternal home. Each day that you spend with me is preparation for that day when you will receive your eternal reward. This indeed is rich bounty.

Live today in the light of these truths. Spend time with me to be reminded of my love and my goodness.

This psalm offers us great comfort when we face death—either our own or that of someone we love dearly. It assures us that God will watch over us even in death. He cares deeply when his loved ones die, and offers us the certain hope of eternal life.

May
3

PSALM 118

Give thanks to the Lord, for he is good! His faithful love endures forever.
– Psalm 118:1

I am good, and my steadfast love endures forever. Repeat that to yourself; let it be a refrain that runs endlessly in the back of your mind as you go about your day. Proclaim this precious reality to others. So many of your questions and struggles are answered by this simple truth: I am good, and my steadfast love lasts for eternity.

I am on your side, so there is no reason to fear. What can anyone do to you with me as your helper? Trust in me, not in people or rulers, for I am your refuge, your strength, your song.

Because of what I have done for you, you can sing glad songs of victory. I have opened to you the gates of righteousness; you can come in and be washed clean of all your sin. Rejoice in the salvation I have wrought for you and bask in my light. I am indeed good, and my steadfast love endures forever.

The repeated refrain of verses 2 through 4 is one we would do well to repeat to ourselves throughout the day: His faithful love endures forever. When troubles come at us, his faithful love endures. When we are afraid or in distress, his faithful love endures.

PSALM 119:1-24

Joyful are those who obey his laws and search for him with all their hearts.

– Psalm 119:2

Do you want to see even greater blessing in your life? Walk in my ways. Seek me with your whole heart, steadfastly devoting yourself to my Word. Then your eyes will be fixed on me and you will be able to worship me with an upright heart.

Do you wish to keep your way pure? Guard your heart with my Word. Do not wander from my commandments. Store my Word in your heart—treasure it, meditate on it, and speak it to others.

If you live this way, you will see wondrous things. I will reveal myself to you in new and exciting ways. Each time you open my Word you will find new treasure there, and your perspective will be molded by eternal truths so that you can live with courage and purpose throughout your earthly journey.

There is a common misconception that the Christian life consists of a bunch of rules designed to take all the fun out of life. These verses remind us that it is a joy to obey God. His ways are the best, and following him will bring us peace both in this life and in the life to come.

May
5

PSALM 119:25-50

Turn my eyes from worthless things, and give me life through your word.
– Psalm 119:37

When your soul is barely clinging to life and your faith is hanging by a thread, open your Bible. There you will find life. I will tell you of my ways and help you understand my thoughts. My words will give you strength and help you live with courage and hope.

Run in the direction of my commands, eagerly seeking my will, and your heart will be enlarged. You will discover my great love for you, and it will spill over into love for those around you. Delight yourself in Scripture and you will find truth and hope. You will not wonder about my will for you—you will know my heart so well from studying my Word that the path before you will be clear.

My Word is truth and hope and life. Meet me in the pages of the Bible and you will be renewed.

The things this world so highly values—power, prestige, comfort, and wealth—are in the end worthless. True life is found in God alone, and we find him in the pages of his Word. Turn away from worthless things and spend time today reading and meditating on the words of life.

PSALM 119:89-112

Your word is a lamp to guide my feet and a light for my path.

– Psalm 119:105

My Word is firmly fixed in the heavens. I established the earth and continually sustain it in faithfulness. I know all things and do all things.

Delight yourself in holy Scripture and you will be spared much sorrow. You will know that I love you and will learn wisdom to live well, so that no one will be able to stand against you. My Word is a lamp to your feet, showing you the next step. It is a light for your path, revealing your hope for the future. What joy you will find in learning my testimonies. They are life for you.

When life feels confusing, return to my Word. It is true and will give you understanding of my ways and my desires for you. It will keep your eyes focused on the truth so that you are not distressed by life's temporary trials.

One thing spending time in God's Word gives us is perspective. There we are reminded of who he is and who we are—and that knowledge helps us live for eternity rather than for temporary pleasures. When life feels confusing or out of control, turn to the pages of Scripture and reorient yourself according to the truth you find there.

PSALM 120

I took my troubles to the LORD; I cried
out to him, and he answered my prayer.

– P s a l m 1 2 0 : 1

My child, call on me when you are distressed. Don't go to your friends or your coping mechanisms. They may mislead you, making you think you can run away from the pain or numb yourself from it. But when you come to me, I will answer you and save you. I will show you truth. My presence brings deep peace to your soul—regardless of circumstances.

People may deceive you to stir up war. They love to make trouble and want to trample on the feelings of others. Life is hard around such people; don't live in their shadow.

Choose instead to associate with those who love peace. Choose friends who point you toward me and my truth. Choose people who bring calm and contentment to your heart. These are the ones who will grow your soul toward life and godliness.

The psalmist was troubled on his pilgrimage through life by all the evil around him. You can probably relate to that. Do what the psalmist did: Turn to God in prayer, and then look for friends who will point you back to God.

May
8

PSALM 121

He who watches over Israel never slumbers or sleeps. The LORD himself
watches over you! The LORD stands beside you as your protective shade.

– P s a l m 1 2 1 : 4 - 5

L ook up at the hills. Does your help come from there? Look to the left and the right—does your help come from the people around you? No! I am your help, the one who made heaven and earth. I can do all things, and I use my power to protect you.

I will not let your foot be moved. I never sleep—I am always taking care of you, each moment of your life. I am your keeper, the shade to protect you from every danger. The threats in the day and the fears of the night cannot touch you, for I am with you.

No evil can come near you, for I am protecting you. I will keep your life. Your comings and goings for all eternity are in my hand.

Children take great comfort in knowing that Mom and Dad are nearby when they sleep, especially when they have a nightmare or there is a thunderstorm. That same feeling of security is ours when we trust in God—he never sleeps and is always watching over us.

May
9

PSALM 122

I was glad when they said to me, "Let us go to the house of the LORD."
– Psalm 122:1

What a privilege it is to have fellowship with others who love me. Enter your house of worship with joy, realizing what a wonderful thing it is to be encouraged by the faith of others. Appreciate the gift it is to have Christian brothers and sisters—imperfect though they are—to walk the journey of life with you.

Your spiritual family is even bigger than you think; you are bound together with all believers around the world. One day people from every tribe and tongue and nation will gather around my throne. Until that day, serve one another in love. Give thanks for the diversity that exists in the family of God. Pray for the peace of other believers and give to meet their needs. Bring my Kingdom to earth now by seeking good for every believer and caring for one another's needs.

Belonging to the body of Christ on earth—the church—is sometimes difficult and messy. But God has created the church to reveal his glory to the nations, and for this reason he commands us to work for the peace and prosperity of our local body of believers. How can you strengthen the fellowship and help it more closely reflect the image of God?

May
10

PSALM 123

I lift my eyes to you, O God, enthroned in heaven.
– Psalm 123:1

Lift your gaze off your problems and onto me. See me seated on my throne, and all your cares will grow pale in the light of my power and holiness. Take time each day to gain perspective on how big I am and you will see how small everything else is.

A servant gazes intently at his master, paying careful attention so he or she can anticipate the master's needs and respond immediately. When you look at me with that kind of focused expectancy, you will be able to anticipate my mercy. You will see how I am loving you and helping you and you will begin to trust me to keep on caring for you. You will notice the moments I lift my hand to bring you aid. Your faith and hope will grow as you gaze on me, for you will see things as they really are.

Is your gaze more often fixed on God or on your life here on earth? As you go about your day, find ways to remind yourself to look at God, seated on his throne.

May
11

PSALM 124

Our help is from the LORD, who made heaven and earth.

– Psalm 124:8

If I were not on your side, you could not have victory over sin and death. Your enemies would have their way. You would live in constant defeat, for without me, you are helpless and hopeless.

But since I am for you, you have nothing to fear. The floods that threaten to sweep you away will be pushed back by my strong hand. The raging waters that surge around you will be silenced with one word.

Your helper is the Lord who made heaven and earth. All power belongs to me, so with me, all things are possible. Why do you fret and fear? Trust me each moment, for I am the God who saves you and you are safe in my arms.

King David, the author of this psalm, knew that no matter how much they strategized, or how strong their army was, Israel could not survive without God's help. That's the position we are in too. We need God's help each day, even for our next breath. Today, look for all the ways God helps you and thank him for them.

May
12

PSALM 125

Those who trust in the LORD are as secure as Mount Zion;
they will not be defeated but will endure forever.

– Psalm 125:1

When you put your trust in me, you made an eternal choice. Your future is secure because you have tuned your heart to mine. I cover you with my faithful loving-kindness. I do good to you, for you belong to me. All my promises are for you, and I will be with you and do what is best for you all the days of your life.

Keep following my ways and you will find rest and peace. Stay close to me so you can sense my love and enjoy abundant blessing. Like a mountain, I tower over you and surround you with my protection. I keep you safe from temptations within and dangers without. Turn to me in your time of need and trust me to take care of you.

As the pilgrims of Israel journeyed to Jerusalem, they sang this song of confidence in God. These promises that God will protect you and do good to you will give you courage and hope as you journey through life toward heaven.

PSALM 126

Restore our fortunes, Lord, as streams renew the desert.
Those who plant in tears will harvest with shouts of joy.

– Psalm 126:4-5

You've seen my mercy in the lives of others, and you wonder when it will be your turn. Their lives seem like a dream; it doesn't look as if they have any problems. I've done great things for them and blessed them, and you wish I would do the same for you.

Don't worry, I am doing good for you also. Those who sow in tears will reap with shouts of joy. Weeping lasts for the night, but joy comes in the morning. I am the God of restoration, redemption, and healing. Wait in expectant hope for the day when your faith shall be sight.

I have promised blessing, so you can be sure it will come. Wait for my joy—eternal blessing in heaven and even joy in this life. Be of good cheer; good things are in store for you.

When the Israelites returned from captivity in Babylon, they sang this song. God had brought them back, but they wanted more. So they prayed for restoration. As you look at the things in your life that haven't gone according to plan, ask God to bring you harvests of joy and restore what has been lost, according to his good plan.

PSALM 127

Unless the LORD builds a house, the work of the builders is wasted.
Unless the LORD protects a city, guarding it with sentries will do no good.

– Psalm 127:1

There's a natural human longing for purpose, for meaningful work and a lasting legacy. The secret for achieving that is to stay close to me.

Without me, your toil is in vain. Your work will come to nothing of lasting value. Apart from me, all your early rising and sleepless nights bring nothing but anxiety.

On the other hand, with me, you will discover your true purpose. You will understand what is truly important so you can invest in things that will last for eternity. Each night you will rest, knowing that you have glorified me that day. Even the tasks you didn't get done will not disturb your sleep because you will know that you will always enough time in a day to accomplish what I am asking you to do. My yoke is easy and my burden is light. Rest as you trust that I am enough for you.

This psalm offers us a blueprint for living a life that really matters. Let God determine your priorities; trust him to build your life according to his plan. Your only job is to follow where he leads, and he will give you fulfillment and rest.

May
15

PSALM 128

How joyful are those who fear the Lord—all who follow his ways!

– Psalm 128:1

See all the ways I have blessed you. You have more than enough to eat. You have meaningful work that glorifies me. Your family is fruitful, and all is well with your soul.

These blessings are not just for you! Share with others. Make sure your neighbors have enough to eat and warm clothes to wear. Bless others by inviting them into the peace of your home. Notice the needs around you and try to help.

This is how I care for my people—by giving you peace and material blessings to share with others. I have blessed you abundantly, so now you can give with generous abandon. Don't hold back, for I have not withheld any good thing from you.

How has God blessed you this week? Find ways to share that blessing with others, whether it is an encouraging word, extra time to offer a helping hand, or an unexpected gift of money that you can give to someone in need.

May 16

PSALM 130

I am counting on the LORD; yes, I am counting
on him. I have put my hope in his word.

– Psalm 130:5

From your deep pit of despair, cry out to me. I hear you. I am attentive to your cry. I am alert, anticipating your summons like a mother waits for her baby's cry.

I don't count your sins, for you have complete and full forgiveness in me. You can stand with confidence before me, for my righteousness covers you.

Wait for me. Hope in my Word. Anticipate my response like a watchman waits for the morning—with eager expectancy. Don't be surprised when I speak to you; be ready for it. With me is steadfast love and plentiful redemption. Hope in me, and you will never be disappointed.

We should pray with expectation that God hears us and will answer us, because he has promised that he will. Count on him for forgiveness and for everlasting hope.

May 17

PSALM 131

I have calmed and quieted myself, like a weaned child who no longer cries for its mother's milk. Yes, like a weaned child is my soul within me.

– Psalm 131:2

Come, child, and sit quietly with me. Be like a weaned child with its mother, not grasping and needy, but calm and trusting. Rest contentedly even when you have questions and doubts and urgent needs.

This is the way of humility: Acknowledge that I am God, and you are not. Sit with trusting confidence, knowing that because I am with you, everything is okay. Things may not look okay, but you know who your tender heavenly Father is, and so you can rest, settled in your soul, casting aside your doubts and fears as you trust in me.

Come, be calm with me. I will soothe your soul and give you peace as only I can.

Think of prayer as sitting with God. Feel his powerful and comforting presence. Don't ask for anything, just calm yourself and be with him. When you start your prayer time this way, your requests begin to feel less urgent and you can confidently leave your concerns with him, trusting that he knows best and will do good to you.

PSALM 132

"This is my resting place forever," he said.
"I will live here, for this is the home I desired."

– Psalm 132:14

My resting place—my home—has always been with my people. I lived in the Tabernacle, and then the Temple, to show my people how much I longed to be with them. These houses of worship were signs of my love.

Then I came as Immanuel, God with us, to be with you and save you. I took on flesh and sinew to experience all that you experience. Now I dwell in your heart, empowering you and sanctifying you. You are my temple! That is how much I desire to be with you and abide with you.

Won't you let me take ownership of every part of you? Let me clothe you with salvation and spread my light into every corner of your being.

Let me fill you with my presence so that you can shout for joy.

When humankind sinned against God, the open relationship between God and humanity was severed. Ever since then, God has been working his purposes to provide a way for us to be with him once again. Meditate on how great God's love is that he longed to be with us that much, and enjoy the relationship you have with him through Christ.

PSALM 133

How wonderful and pleasant it is when brothers live together in harmony!

– Psalm 133:1

My church should be a place of unity, not division. You should be one with your brothers and sisters in the faith just as I am one with the Son, vitally connected in love to save many. How good and pleasant it is when you live in unity—it is my blessing on you.

Don't let petty differences divide what I have declared is one body. Seek peace with one another. Remind each other of your common purpose. Appreciate that one person is a hand and another is a foot, and both are needed. Then learn to work together so that my purposes are accomplished in the world. The church is my instrument of blessing in the world; don't hinder that through disunity.

God's intention is that all believers are united as one body, just as God the Father and God the Son are united. Has that been your experience? How can you work to achieve that kind of unity with your brothers and sisters in the church?

May
20

PSALM 135

Your name, O LORD, endures forever; your fame,
O LORD, is known to every generation.

– Psalm 135:13

Y ou are chosen. I redeemed you—at great cost—for my own possession. I did this not because you deserved it, but because it pleased
me—because I am love.

I am above all gods. I make the clouds rise and lightning strike. The
wind comes from my storehouses. I bring down rulers and raise them up.
I redeem and restore with compassion. Yes, my name and my purposes
endure forever.

And I have chosen you. Won't you choose me as well? Leave behind
the worthless idols, those false gods who can't speak or see or act. Worship
me, the true God who lives and works on your behalf. See how beloved
you are and respond by giving yourself to me.

There is a striking contrast between the living, active God who
redeems his people and the lifeless idols that people choose
instead of him. The truth is, we become like what we worship.
Do your actions demonstrate that you serve the living God, or
have you inadvertently begun to serve worthless things that lead
to death?

May
21

PSALM 136

Give thanks to the God of heaven. His faithful love endures forever.

– P s a l m   1 3 6 : 2 6

What can you thank me for?

I am good—the very definition of all that is good.

My steadfast love endures forever.

I do great wonders, even more than you can see or imagine.

I made the heavens and spread out the earth. I made sun, moon, and stars—and you!

I save my people with a strong hand, calling forth life from what is broken and worthless.

I make a way through the sea so you can pass through unharmed. I strike down kings, for I am above every earthly authority.

I give you an inheritance that is eternal, imperishable, and undefiled.

And I remember you in your humble position, giving you all you need now and for eternity.

What else can you thank me for?

Make a list of all the things you can thank God for today, and recite the words his "faithful love endures forever" after each one to remind yourself that it is God's unfailing love that causes him to bless you in these ways.

PSALM 137

How can we sing the songs of the LORD while in a pagan land?

- Psalm 137:4

A stranger in the land, alone and in despair, you cry out to me. You feel as though I have abandoned you. You wonder if you will ever be able to sing again. You didn't choose this place, and you don't want to be here. How can you worship me in such a terrible place?

I have not forgotten you. You are my joy, and I will save you so that you can praise me again. Yes, you will once again sing joyful songs.

My greatest happiness is in doing good for you, and that is what I am doing. So don't give up hope. Joy is coming—just wait for it. I will never leave you or forget you, and I am always working things out for your good.

No matter where you are today, how far you feel from God, or how much evil surrounds you, you can sing songs to the Lord, just as the Jews in exile did. Find a song to sing today—even if you are in such a dark place that all you can do is hum along to someone else's song.

PSALM 138

As soon as I pray, you answer me; you encourage me by giving me strength.

– P s a l m   1 3 8 : 3

When you give your heart to worship, honoring me for my steadfast love and faithfulness, your soul will be strengthened. In the simple act of praising me, I will remind you of all the ways I care for you.

Though you walk through troubles, I preserve your life. I stretch out my hand to save you from every threat. I provide for you, bending down from my throne to care for everything that concerns you.

Take courage: I will fulfill my purposes for you. I will never forsake the work of my hands, but will complete what I have begun. My steadfast love endures forever and my faithfulness continues through all generations— for you and for those who come after you.

Sometimes it takes great courage to say the psalmist's words: "The LORD will work out his plans for my life." But that is the truth. Whatever is happening to you, God is at work. Trust that he cares for you and will save you.

PSALM 139:1-12

You go before me and follow me. You place your hand of blessing on my head.

– Psalm 139:5

I know everything about you. I know when you sit down and when you get up. I discern every thought you have. I prepare your paths and am acquainted with all your habits. I know what you are going to say before you even form the thought. I know all this, and yet I still love you.

I place my hand of protection on you. Try as you might, you can never escape my Spirit or flee from my presence. I am everywhere, filling heaven and earth! And that means I am always holding you in my hand, day and night.

Lean into that truth and let it give you peace—I, the God who knows you and loves you, am always with you.

When life is confusing or you feel alone, you can find comfort in remembering that God knows everything about you. Nothing escapes his notice, and he cares for each detail of your life. Thank God for knowing you and loving you in this way.

PSALM 139:13-24

You saw me before I was born. Every day of my life was recorded in your book. Every moment was laid out before a single day had passed.

– Psalm 139:16

I am your Creator. Every part of you was lovingly knit together by my hands. You are fearfully and wonderfully made, lovely and beautiful in my sight. Everything about you I have declared to be very good.

Don't belittle or speak badly of what I have made and what I have declared to be good. Don't demean or criticize yourself. Instead, see yourself through my eyes. I love every quirk about you, and I put it there for a reason.

Live with the sweet knowledge that I have planned all of your days just for you! I made you with a purpose. I will help you discover it and live it if you follow me.

There is a lot of talk these days about self-esteem and identity. For the believer, our identity and our confidence lie in the fact that God made each of us with a purpose, and he is working out those purposes. Let God define you as his beloved child, and let the knowledge that you are known and loved by your Creator give you confidence to do anything he calls you to do.

May 26

PSALM 141

Accept my prayer as incense offered to you,
and my upraised hands as an evening offering.

– Psalm 141:2

When you call to me, I come running. I hear your voice and incline my ear to listen to your words. Your prayers rise up before me as a sweet aroma, and I draw near to you as you worship me. In those quiet moments together, so many things are happening.

I set a guard around you, protecting you from careless words. I incline your heart toward good and strengthen you to obey me. I make your heart soft and humble toward my correction.

Lift up your eyes to me so I can be your refuge. Let me protect you from the dangers even of your own heart. Come near so I can enfold you in my protective embrace.

Even your urgent prayers for help can be offered up as a fragrant incense before God's throne. He loves it when you bring your needs to him. As you pray for help, keep in your mind that image of upraised hands bringing an offering to God.

PSALM 142

When I am overwhelmed, you alone know the way I should turn.

– Psalm 142:3

Bring your complaints to me. Tell me your troubles. I see that your spirit is faint. You aren't sure what to do next because there seem to be land mines everywhere you turn. Every option before you is fraught with potential danger. No one seems to care what happens to you.

I care. I am your refuge. I am your portion, and I am more than enough. Your problems may be too big for you, but they are not too big for me. I will free you from the thoughts that imprison you and give you of my bounty. Come to me and see that I am all you need.

David wrote these words in a cave, hiding out from his enemies. He needed God's help literally to know where to go, because a wrong turn would probably lead to death. If you feel trapped today, not sure where to go next, ask God to help you. He will bring you out of your difficulty so that you can once again thank him for his goodness.

PSALM 143

Come quickly, LORD, and answer me, for my
depression deepens. Don't turn away from me, or I will die.

– Psalm 143:7

In these days of crushing darkness, when your soul feels like a parched and barren wilderness, remember the days that came before. Meditate on what I have done. Ponder my works of faithfulness and righteousness. Think on the good days and trust that you will experience more of them.

In your time of need, stretch out your hands and bring your thirsty soul to drink of me, the fount of living water. I will answer you. I will not hide my face from you. In the morning I will remind you of my steadfast love. I will show you the way to go and lift up your soul from the depths.

I am your refuge, your deliverer, and your guide. Come, follow me into hope and light.

This psalm is the prayer of a depressed man; he is so distressed that he is afraid he will die. But even in this state he runs to God for help. If you are in distress, join in this prayer that God will place you on firm footing for his own glory.

May
29

PSALM 144

He is my loving ally and my fortress, my tower of safety,
my rescuer. He is my shield, and I take refuge in him.

– Psalm 144:2

Everyone is trying to find solid ground in these days of chaos and difficulty. What they are really looking for is what you have already found—me. I am the rock. I am your steadfast fortress and your stronghold for the day of trouble.

The days of a person's life on earth are few, like a passing shadow. But my love is forever. I take note of you and reach down from heaven to take care of you. I reach out and rescue you from the deep waters by my strong hand.

Sing a new song to me. I bring victory and abundance—sing about that. I bless you with strength and provision. You are indeed blessed, for you have the God of heaven and earth as your foundation forever.

Life is short and insignificant, but God gives us purpose. He prepares us for our work (verse 1) and comes down to rescue his people. This dual reality of God's sovereign will and our responsibility to live well the life he has given us is found throughout Scripture, and it gives dignity to our daily tasks of taking care of our families and making a living (verses 12-14).

PSALM 145:1-13

Everyone will share the story of your wonderful goodness;
they will sing with joy about your righteousness.

– Psalm 145:7

You have so many ways and so many reasons to praise me. The vocabulary of worship is deep and rich. So use it all! Summon all your resources, all your knowledge, all your talents to bless my name and praise me for my unsearchable greatness.

Tell my works to the next generation. Meditate on my wondrous works. Declare my greatness and pour forth the fame of my abundant goodness. Sing aloud of my righteousness.

For I am gracious and merciful, slow to get angry and overflowing with steadfast love. I pour out mercy on all I have made. Behold, I am faithful and true in all I do. Let your praises ring out this day and every day.

There are so many reasons and so many ways to praise the Lord. Think of ways you can proclaim his greatness to someone today—and then be sure to do it!

PSALM 145:14-20

*The L**ORD** is close to all who call on him, yes, to all who call on him in truth. He grants the desires of those who fear him; he hears their cries for help and rescues them.*

– Psalm 145:18-19

Notice my kindness to you and to everything I have made. Yes, there is evil, but my kindness and mercy are evident throughout the earth as well.

I uphold those who are falling and raise up those who are bowed down by trouble and grief. I give food to those who trust in me. I open my hand at just the moment my generosity is needed, and not a moment sooner. I satisfy the desires of every living thing with myself.

I am righteous in my ways and kind in my works. Best of all, I am near. When you cry out in sincerity of heart, I am right beside you. I fulfill your desires and hear your cries. I save and preserve you in your time of need. This day, with all of its worries and cares, choose to trust me. I take care of those who are mine.

Theologians call it common grace—the care God shows to each of his creatures and the way he brings rain on the just and the unjust (see Matthew 5:45). Praise God for all the ways he shows his kindness to the earth, to those who have rejected him and to those who love him.

June

June

1

PSALM 146

*Joyful are those who have the God of Israel as their
helper, whose hope is in the L*ORD *their God.*

– Psalm 146:5

Dear one, where are you placing your trust? Do you trust in your leaders to save you and prosper you? Do you count on your friends to help you? They will surely disappoint, for they are flawed mortals.

But if you trust in me, placing your hope in my sure promises, you will not be disappointed. I am the creator of heaven and earth. I am the one who works justice and righteousness. I feed the hungry and care for the oppressed. I set prisoners free and give sight to the blind. I uphold the widows and orphans and bring ruin to those who seek to harm others.

I reign over all, and my Kingdom will continue forever. Trust in me. Rest in the knowledge that I am doing good for you all the days of your life.

People will always let us down in one way or another, because no one is perfect. But God never lets us down. That is why we can have joy in any circumstance—because we know that the God of the universe is our helper.

PSALM 147

*The LORD's delight is in those who fear him,
those who put their hope in his unfailing love.*

– Psalm 147:11

It is fitting to worship me. Think on all I have done! I created the stars and call them by name, yet I draw near to gather outcasts to myself and bind up broken hearts. I lift up the humble and cast down the proud. I care so much for you that I use my abundant power and unfathomable understanding to work in your world, to care for the things that concern you.

Sing with thanksgiving. I, the Creator and Lord of all, make the rain to fall and the grass to grow—yet my true delight is in you. I strengthen and bless you. I give you peace and prosperity. I send out my Word to help you. The almighty God of the universe cares for you!

You might think that God who counts the stars and calls them by name, who brings rain and feeds the animals, wouldn't be concerned about sinful humans who reject him over and over. Yet God cares for our wounds when we are brokenhearted, and he delights in us. That is something to praise him for, and should make us eager to obey him.

PSALMS 148—150

Let everything that breathes sing praises to the LORD! Praise the LORD!

- Psalm 150:6

It is always the right time to sing to me and praise my name. Even if your heart is weighed down and everything is going wrong, I am still worthy of all praise and glory. Worship me for the wonders of creation. Exalt me for my glory and majesty. Praise me for my past faithfulness.

I will put a new song in your heart. You will once again tell others of my greatness, for you will be so amazed at what I have done that you can't keep it in.

This day, with all its troubles, put your faith in my character and praise me anyway. Bring your mumbled, broken hallelujahs to me. Then wait and see what I will do, for I delight in adorning humble people with salvation.

It is fitting that the book of Psalms ends with these psalms of praise. That is what we are to be about, every day of our lives—praising the God who made us, redeemed us, and loves us.

EXODUS 20

I am the LORD your God, who rescued you from the land of Egypt,
the place of your slavery. You must not have any other god but me.

– E x o d u s   2 0 : 2 - 3

Some days I just remind you of my love, but some days you need to be reminded of my will for you—my laws that teach you what pleases me.

Love me more than anything or anyone else. Make me your first priority, and don't worship anything besides me. Revere me and keep my name holy. Trust me enough to cease your striving and rest on the Sabbath. Honor and serve your parents, for they are my gift to you. Don't murder or hate the people I have made. Keep marriage pure and holy. Do not take what isn't yours. Speak the truth at all times, even when a lie would be more convenient. Be content with what I have given you—don't covet what I have given to someone else.

If you truly love me, you will keep my commandments.

The apostle John told us that we can measure our love for God by our obedience to him (see John 14:15). We don't obey to make God love us—he already does. Nor do we obey to earn our salvation—we never could deserve it. Rather, we submit to him out of love. Do you love God enough to do what he asks?

EXODUS 23

*See, I am sending an angel before you to protect you on your
journey and lead you safely to the place I have prepared for you.*

– E x o d u s   2 3 : 2 0

You can trust me to do what is right and good. What I have given you is enough, and you can find joyful rest in my provision.

One way you do that is by resting when I have told you to rest. Don't work seven days a week—trust that I will provide all you need in six days. The rest of a quiet Sunday afternoon is my gift to you.

You can also rest by letting me establish your borders. Entrust the increase of your business to me—I will give you everything you need to accomplish my purposes. Trust me to show you the right place to live, the right church, the right friends. Pray about these things and then leave them up to me by following my lead. I will bring you to the place I have prepared for you.

People sometimes think the Old Testament laws are archaic. But each of the laws in this chapter has a modern-day application for our lives—commands to be honest, to trust God to meet our needs, and to be careful to obey him. Woven through it all is an invitation into deeper trust and rest in the God who goes before us to lead us.

EXODUS 25—27

*Have the people of Israel build me a holy sanctuary so I can
live among them. You must build this Tabernacle and its
furnishings exactly according to the pattern I will show you.*

– E x o d u s   2 5 : 8 - 9

In days of old, I established my worship, declaring how everything was to be made and done. In great detail I decreed the specifications for the Tabernacle, a place of beauty where people could come near to me. I was showing you my holiness.

Now you can enter my presence freely by trusting the blood of Jesus, the perfect Lamb of God, to save you. The sacrifices and rituals are gone, and freedom is here. This is relationship, not ritual. Love, not legalism.

But I'm still the same God who commanded my people to build the Tabernacle just so, and that means I must be worshiped on my terms. Come to me with a sincere heart. Worship in Spirit and in truth. Trust Jesus alone, not your own deeds of righteousness. Then you can worship me with a heart that is cleansed and purified and whole!

We are often tempted to create God in our image and worship him on our terms. These chapters remind us of God's holiness and call us to reverent awe at God's glory.

EXODUS 28–29

I will live among the people of Israel and be their God, and they will know that I am the LORD their God. I am the one who brought them out of the land of Egypt so that I could live among them. I am the LORD their God.

– Exodus 29:45-46

Aaron and all the Levitical priests after him had to purify themselves and put on holy garments to enter my presence. They were acknowledging my holiness and their unworthiness.

I still require robes of righteousness, but now I give them to anyone who washes in my blood. Whoever relies by faith in my sacrifice to save them from sin is cleansed from every impurity and is given a white robe. They can enter my presence and worship me in the splendor of holiness.

So consecrate yourself to me. Trust in me alone for salvation and dedicate yourself to worshiping me in every area of life. Wash your heart clean through repentance. Then you can enter my presence fully worthy of my love—worthy because I have made you righteous.

When we read about all the requirements for approaching God in the Old Testament, it's a relief to remember that we come before him with confidence, anytime we want. Jesus broke down the dividing wall between God and his people, and now we ourselves are the temple of the Holy Spirit, the place where God dwells.

June

8

EXODUS 33

*As my glorious presence passes by, I will hide you in the crevice
of the rock and cover you with my hand until I have passed by.*

– E x o d u s   3 3 : 2 2

Just like Moses, you long to see my glory. You know of my greatness, but you are so easily distracted by the shine of the world that you lose sight of my glory. You stumble in the darkness rather than walking in my light.

You can always see my goodness, for each day it passes before you. I am gracious to you and show you mercy. I proclaim over and over in your life that I am God, and I love you. I meet your needs and answer your prayers—all this grace is a taste of my goodness.

But I protect you from the full weight of my glory, because no one can look on me and live. So gaze on me, marvel at my goodness, but know that this is but a shadow of my glory. Your great hope and joy are found in the truth that one day you will live in my eternal glory, experiencing my full brightness forever.

We see God's glory all around us, in the world he has made and in the people he has created and redeemed. But all of this is just a foretaste of his greatness, which we will see in full when he gives us new bodies in heaven, bodies that can bear the weight of his glory.

LEVITICUS 26:1-13

*I am the LORD your God, who brought you out of the land of
Egypt so you would no longer be their slaves. I broke the yoke of
slavery from your neck so you can walk with your heads held high.*

– Leviticus 26:13

Your actions and choices have consequences. If you walk in my ways,
things will go well for you. The rains will come in due season and the
land will yield its increase. Your work will bear fruit, and you will have
everything you need.

Best of all, you will have peace in your heart and in your life. Your
relationships will be calm, and no one will be able to speak badly of you. I
will be close to you, for there will be no bitterness and sin creating a wall
between us.

You are my child, and I am your God. I fight for you and bring good
to you all the days of your life. I have broken the curse of sin and death so
you can truly live—having eternal, abundant life in me.

God broke the yoke of our slavery to sin so that we can be free
to obey him, free to say no to the darkness. Make a conscious
effort today to exercise your freedom to say no to sin and yes to
God, and then see how each of those right choices leads to good
things in your life.

June
10

LEVITICUS 26:14-45

*Despite all this, I will not utterly reject or despise
them. . . . I will not cancel my covenant with them.*

– Leviticus 26:44

All my promises are for you if you follow me, but if you choose to serve other gods instead of me, life will not go well for you.

Your life will be characterized by panic, by wasting diseases and heartache and anxiety. Your work will not bring the results you hope for. You will be ruled by people who hate you. One day your pride will be broken.

You see, my discipline falls on those who despise me. I discipline in order that they will turn to me. So come willingly. Serve me now so my hand doesn't have to deal harshly with you to bring you back to the path of life. Return to me and live! Repent, and I will once again pour my blessing out on you.

Our sinful choices have consequences, and God often disciplines us when we do wrong. But he does it in love, for he remembers his covenant promises to save us, and he never goes back on his word. Choose today to obey God so that you will not have to suffer his hand of discipline.

NUMBERS 9:15-23

*They traveled and camped at the LORD's command
wherever he told them to go. Then they remained in their
camp as long as the cloud stayed over the Tabernacle.*

– Numbers 9:18

In the Exodus I led my people visibly—with a pillar of cloud by day and a pillar of fire by night. Even people who didn't know me could see how I loved and led my people. Sometimes for days on end I would tell them to stay; other times we would move again and again, never getting too comfortable in one spot.

That is the way I lead you, too, if you're looking for it. My leading is visible. I don't hide my will from you—I want you to find it! If you can't tell where I'm leading, stay where you are and wait on me. The times of sameness and stability are no less part of my leading than the times of motion.

Trust me to clearly lead you in my will, to lead you so powerfully that even people who don't know me will see it and be amazed.

If you ask God to lead you, he will. You may have to wait where you are for a little longer—he doesn't reveal himself on our timetable—but those times of waiting are often the times when our faith grows the most.

NUMBERS 14

Do not rebel against the LORD, and don't be afraid of the people of the land. They are only helpless prey to us! They have no protection, but the LORD is with us! Don't be afraid of them!

– Numbers 14:9

I hear you grumbling like the Israelites of old, thinking maybe life would be easier apart from me. The task before you seems too big. The giants are intimidating. You don't think you're up to the job and wonder if I have the wrong person, or if you heard me wrong. The life you had in Egypt wasn't perfect, but at least it was familiar. Comfortable. Predictable. Going back seems preferable to moving forward.

Believe in me. Remember all the wonders you have seen me perform, and take courage. I am filling the earth with my glory—don't doubt my purposes or my methods. Trust my plan, and don't grumble in unbelief.

The task I have given you may be too big for you, but it is not too big for me. I will help you overtake all the giants in the land. I go before you to prepare the way, and all my paths are peace and wisdom. Only believe and do not fear.

Do you ever wonder what would have happened if the Israelites had trusted God instead of doubting his promises? Forty years of difficulty and death could have been avoided. What is God asking you to trust him for today? Save yourself the heartache of doubt and choose instead to believe that he is with you and will fight for you.

NUMBERS 23:19; 24:17-19

God is not a man, so he does not lie. He is not human,
so he does not change his mind. Has he ever spoken and failed
to act? Has he ever promised and not carried it through?

– Numbers 23:19

You are made in my image, not the other way around. I do not lie or change like a shifting shadow. You do not have to worry that I am in a bad mood—I am from everlasting to everlasting the same. My will stands eternal in the heavens, and what I say, I will do.

My people learned this in the way I kept my promise through the ages to send a deliverer. All through the Old Testament I promised to send a King to crush the evil one. Now you have seen him and know him—Jesus the Messiah, your rescuer. He won the victory once and for all. My will was accomplished as I had promised.

So this day, take courage and comfort in the fact that I am the same yesterday, today, and forever. Ever loving you, ever faithful to you, always good.

What a comfort it is to know that God is not like us. He is not fickle or capricious or unpredictable. What he says, he will do. His character is consistent from eternity past to eternity future. You can depend on him.

DEUTERONOMY 1:28-31

*Don't be shocked or afraid of them! The LORD your God is going
ahead of you. He will fight for you, just as you saw him do in Egypt.
And you saw how the LORD your God cared for you all along
the way as you traveled through the wilderness, just as a father
cares for his child. Now he has brought you to this place.*

– Deuteronomy 1:29-31

What I have commanded you to do, I will give you all you need to accomplish. There may be giants in the land. The sight of the obstacles in your path may make your heart melt. But I say to you, do not dread the future or be afraid.

I go before you. I myself will fight for you. I will carry you as a father gently bears up his child, the whole journey through your wilderness. In fact, the wilderness is where I meet my people—think of Moses and Hagar and the people of Israel.

Believe that I will do for you in the future as I have done for you in the past. I am still caring for you and loving you steadfastly. I am in your midst, so there is nothing to fear.

> As the Israelites stood at the edge of the Promised Land, they had a lot to be afraid of. They knew that their ancestors had been here before—and had failed. As you stand at the edge of your unknowns, take comfort in the knowledge that your heavenly Father cares for you and has brought you here. He will not leave you.

DEUTERONOMY 4:1-14, 23-24, 31

Do not add to or subtract from these commands I am giving you.
Just obey the commands of the LORD your God that I am giving you.

– D e u t e r o n o m y   4 : 2

I have given you all my holy will in the pages of my Word. Don't try to add to it or subtract from it. Keep my Word, nothing more and nothing less. Do what I say, for my words are life for you.

Keep your soul diligently, lest you forget my goodness and stray from the way of wisdom. Make my ways known to your children and grandchildren. Tell them how I led and cared for you all the days of your life. Teach them of my power and glory, of my holy laws.

Don't forget my covenant. I am a jealous God, eager for your single-hearted devotion to me. If you follow after other gods, I will do all it takes to call you back, for I love you and want you for my own.

One of the challenges that faces us as believers is correctly applying God's Word to our lives. We need to obey what God has commanded without adding our own opinions or rituals (legalism) or lessening its requirements to make it easier to obey (license).

DEUTERONOMY 4:32-40

*Remember this and keep it firmly in mind: The LORD is
God both in heaven and on earth, and there is no other.*

– Deuteronomy 4:39

Is there any other god like me? Does any other god speak out of the fire and let you live? Has anyone else made a nation for himself and led them out by a mighty hand? Has anyone else died to save rebellious creatures? Who but me does such wonders?

I chose you and placed my love on you. I bring you into my presence by my great power, driving out the forces of darkness so you can stand before me, forgiven and whole. I speak to you and show you the way you should go. I give you a glorious inheritance, which I keep in heaven for you.

Dedicate yourself to knowing me as God. Keep my laws so life may go well with you. Remind yourself moment by moment that I am the God of heaven and earth, and I am taking care of you.

You can search all of history, all around the globe, and you will never find another god like the Lord our God. All your longings— for truth and love and forgiveness and life—find their fulfillment in him.

June
17

DEUTERONOMY 6

Listen closely, Israel, and be careful to obey. Then all will go well with you.

– D e u t e r o n o m y   6 : 3

The secret to living well and being wise is to fear me. Reverence me in your heart and humbly submit to me. Fear the judgment of hell more than anything mere mortals can do to you, and obey my commandments. Be careful to do what is right so it will go well with you. Love me above all others, with all your heart and all your soul and all your might.

Teach your children to love me with all their hearts. Talk of me when you sit in your house and when you drive them to their activities, before bed and first thing in the morning. Bind my commandments to your heart and put them before your eyes so you will be reminded of them often.

When you are blessed with a good yield for your work, take care lest you forget me. I am the one who saves you, not your bank account or your job security. Don't chase after other gods. Do what is right and good so you can take possession of all I have for you.

Have you wholeheartedly committed to God? Or are you trying to hold back a piece for yourself? Give everything to him, and he will give you back far more than you gave up—abundant joy and peace for this life and the next.

DEUTERONOMY 7:7-15

*The Lord did not set his heart on you and choose you because you
were more numerous than other nations, for you were the smallest
of all nations! Rather, it was simply that the Lord loves you.*

– D e u t e r o n o m y 7 : 7 - 8

Do you know why I have blessed you so much? Why I have made you
mine? It isn't because you deserved it, or because you were better
than anyone else. No, you are my treasured possession because I set my
love on you and chose you. It was all me, not anything you did.

Know that I am the faithful God who keeps my covenant. Now that I
have chosen you, nothing can pluck you out of my hand. No threat, no
power, nothing in heaven or earth can take away my love for you. Not
even your own rebellion will make me turn my back on you. I have said
that you are mine, and nothing can change that.

Rest in my love and serve me all your days. Trust my provision and
protection, and know that because you have my love, you have everything
you need.

There is a longing deep within us to be chosen. The best news
we could ever receive is that God chose us. It doesn't matter who
else may accept us or reject us, because the creator of the ends
of the earth chose us and loves us.

June

19

DEUTERONOMY 8

Remember how the LORD your God led you through the wilderness for these forty years, humbling you and testing you to prove your character, and to find out whether or not you would obey his commands.

– D e u t e r o n o m y   8 : 2

This test you're going through has a purpose: It has come from my hand for your good—to humble you and reveal what is truly in your heart. Will you keep my commandments even when it is difficult? Will you trust me with everything?

I discipline my children, those whom I love. Just as a father is compelled to turn his children back onto the path of life when they have made a wrong turn, so I guide and lead you because I love you. I am helping you find the good land, the places of life and growth that you can find only by living my way.

True life is found in my Word. Follow it and you will lack no good thing. Let me bless you as you follow me.

Going through trials is hard, and we would do almost anything to avoid them, but it is comforting to know that our difficulties come from the hand of our loving Father, and he does it all for our good. Will you trust him even when it's difficult?

DEUTERONOMY 9

You must recognize that the LORD your God is not giving you this good land because you are good, for you are not—you are a stubborn people.

– Deuteronomy 9:6

The road ahead has its obstacles—I can see that. Mighty warriors stand in your way. But I go before you. I am a consuming fire, and I will subdue all that stands in the way of you doing my will.

When I have accomplished this victory for you, do not say that you did it in your own power. No, I smooth the path ahead of you for my sake. It is in my strength that you go forth and accomplish my purposes.

I pour out victory and blessings on you not because you are righteous, but because I love you. You are stubborn and hard-hearted, determined to sabotage your growth, but I help you grow for my own sake. Rejoice that I love you this much and rest as you let me fight for you.

These words were probably humbling for the Israelites to hear: The battle would be hard, and God wasn't going to give them the land because they deserved it. It does us good to be reminded every now and then about our past failures so we can remember that God saved us by his grace, not because of anything we did. That knowledge frees us up to extend grace to one another.

DEUTERONOMY 10:12-22

What does the LORD your God require of you? He requires only that you fear the LORD your God, and live in a way that pleases him, and love him and serve him with all your heart and soul.

– Deuteronomy 10:12

What am I asking of you? It's simple, really. Fear me as God, walk in my ways, love me, and serve me wholeheartedly. These things I command are not burdensome; they are for your good.

To me belong heaven and earth and everything in them. I am the almighty Creator and King. Yet I set my heart on you in love and chose you. So consecrate yourself to me. Focus your mind on serving me, and do not stubbornly cling to habits of sin and unbelief.

I am the God of gods, the great and mighty, the awesome God. I execute justice and love the sojourner. Hold fast to me and make me the object of your praise. Honor me as your God and see how I will continue to show myself to you.

When it comes right down to it, obeying God isn't very complicated: Love God and love your neighbor. But it isn't easy. Ask God to give you his power to help you obey his simple yet difficult commands.

DEUTERONOMY 11

Commit yourselves wholeheartedly to these words of mine. Tie them to your hands and wear them on your forehead as reminders. Teach them to your children. Talk about them when you are at home and when you are on the road, when you are going to bed and when you are getting up. Write them on the doorposts of your house and on your gates.

– D e u t e r o n o m y   1 1 : 1 8 - 2 0

If you obey my commands, choosing to love and serve me with your heart and soul, you will have joy and peace. Don't be deceived and turn aside to worship other gods. If you do that, I will shut up the heavens so there is no blessing in your life.

Lay up these words of mine in your heart and in your soul. Bind them to your hand and place them before your eyes. Teach them to your children. Talk of them as you go about your day, morning and night. Write them on the walls and doorposts of your house.

If you hold fast to me and are careful to obey, then I will drive out your enemies. You will be blessed with influence and enlarged territory. This is the choice before you: blessing and life if you obey and hardship if you do not. What will you choose?

Moses gave the people practical advice for keeping God's commandments. In modern terms he told them to write verses on Post-it notes and text about them throughout the day so they would be written on their hearts. What do you do to keep God's Word in your heart and mind?

DEUTERONOMY 12

*When you drive out the nations that live there, you must
destroy all the places where they worship their gods.*

– D e u t e r o n o m y   1 2 : 2

The people around you worship everything but me. They run after sex and money. They chase selfish dreams and live only to satisfy their sinful desires. They shrink into obscurity as their world becomes filled with the tiny god of self. Don't be like them.

Tear down the altars to false gods. Erase every trace of them that might turn your heart away from me. Don't make allowances for sinful habits.

Seek me alone. Spend time with me, reading and meditating on my Word. Rejoice in me, living a life of worship. Take pleasure in righteousness, choosing not to do what is right in your own eyes, but rather to obey me. Then you will live in safety and enjoy my blessing.

Moses used violent terms to describe the way the Israelites needed to root sin out of their lives: destroy, break down, smash, burn, completely erase (verses 2-3). He knew they would fall into idol worship if they didn't intentionally avoid it. What will you do to violently uproot the sinful habits, behaviors, thoughts, and attitudes that have crept into your life?

DEUTERONOMY 28

You will experience all these blessings if you obey the LORD your God.

– D e u t e r o n o m y   2 8 : 2

Those who live only for themselves are destined to a life of confusion and frustration. Everything goes wrong for them in the end. They are overthrown by their enemies and live in darkness, far from me.

But those who serve me are blessed. Obey me faithfully, and I will set you in a firm place. You will find purpose and a lasting legacy in your work, for nothing you do in my name is ever in vain. You will have all you need, for I provide for my own. Your enemies will flee before you. I will establish you as my own dear child. Indeed, I will open the heavens and unleash blessings on you.

Choose the life and blessings that come through obedience to my Word.

The covenant God made with Israel was an if/then proposition. If they trusted and obeyed God, then things would go well for them—blessings. If they did not, then things would go badly—curses. We have a choice too: We can choose life in Christ or death in sin. What choice will you make today?

June
25

DEUTERONOMY 29:1-9

*For forty years I led you through the wilderness, yet your
clothes and sandals did not wear out. You ate no bread and
drank no wine or other alcoholic drink, but he provided for
you so you would know that he is the LORD your God.*

– D e u t e r o n o m y   2 9 : 5 - 6

There is a difference between seeing with your eyes and seeing with
your heart. You read in my Word how I led my people through the
wilderness. Their shoes did not wear out. I gave them bread from heaven
and water from a rock. You know all these stories.

But do you see it with your heart? Do you believe I can feed and care
for you? Do you notice all the ways I provide for you and show you my
love? Do you really trust me?

Come and let me reveal to you the depths of my goodness. Trust me
enough not to worry about your needs. Believe that I will keep all my
promises. Put your faith in me for this wilderness, for this need. Then rest
and see with the eyes of your heart how much I love you.

God made an unbreakable covenant promise to take care of
anyone who trusts in him. If you have forsaken the desires of
your own stubborn heart and chosen to follow God—in other
words, if you are a Christian—he has promised to faithfully love
you forever.

DEUTERONOMY 30

The LORD your God will change your heart and the
hearts of all your descendants, so that you will love him
with all your heart and soul and so you may live!

– D e u t e r o n o m y   3 0 : 6

Return to me from all the places you have wandered. Put away your idols and serve me with your whole heart. Let me gather you in from your places of rebellion and doubt. Don't be an outcast anymore—come back home.

Then I will bless you and prosper you. The work of your hands will yield increase. You will hear my voice and sense my delight in you. Obey my commands and you will experience these spiritual blessings in abundance.

The things I ask of you are not difficult. My Word declares all my good will for you. My laws are written in your heart, and the Spirit reminds you of them. Simply love me and love your neighbor. This is life for you, and length of days that you may dwell in peace in the place I am bringing you to.

Even way back in Deuteronomy, God promised that he would replace our hearts of stone with hearts of flesh. The only way we can obey and serve God is if he has given us new birth in Christ, a new heart and a new nature that lives for him.

DEUTERONOMY 32:1-14

He nourished them with honey from the
rock and olive oil from the stony ground.

– Deuteronomy 32:13

L et the heavens ring with my praises. Worship me and proclaim my greatness. My work is perfect and all my ways are just. I am faithful and righteous, upright and holy. I am your Father who created you and established you. I have been faithful to my people through the generations.

I chose you as my inheritance. You were in a desert land, and I came and encircled you in my embrace and cared for you. You are the apple of my eye, my precious beloved. I spread my wings over you like an eagle protectively holds its young under its pinions. I make you fly high over the land and give you honey from the rock—sweetness in hard places. I feed you the finest wheat and wine.

See how great my love is for you, that I care for you so tenderly.

Let the poetry of these verses wash over your soul, reminding you that God cares for you as a loving Father—meeting all your needs in rich abundance.

June

28

DEUTERONOMY 32:15-20, 39-43

You neglected the Rock who had fathered you;
you forgot the God who had given you birth.

– D e u t e r o n o m y 3 2 : 1 8

Despite my tender care for you, you sometimes forsake me. You scoff at the Rock of your salvation. You follow after strange gods. You sacrifice everything to serve your own appetites. You forget me, the God who gave you birth.

See that I am God, and there is none beside me. I kill and bring to life. I wound and I heal. No one can be delivered out of my hand, for I am the righteous judge.

Yet I show compassion on all who love me, even to a thousand generations. I forgive all your iniquities and blot out all your transgressions. It is not too late. Even though you have run far from me, turn back to me, repent, and I will give you life.

God does not want us to share our love with anyone or anything else; he is a jealous God. Are you putting anything before him? Choose today to put him first in your life and in your heart.

DEUTERONOMY 33

How blessed you are, O Israel! Who else is like you, a people saved by the LORD? He is your protecting shield and your triumphant sword!

– Deuteronomy 33:29

I pour out blessing on my people. I shine forth with love for you. You are safe in my care because I surround you all day long and dwell with you and in you.

The choicest gifts of heaven are yours, spiritual blessings beyond imagining: forgiveness and peace and close relationship, life and abundance now and forever.

There is none like me, who rides through the heavens to help you. I am your dwelling place, and underneath you are my everlasting arms. You are the saved of the Lord. I am the shield of your help and the sword of your triumph.

This chapter is the blessing that old father Moses spoke over the people he had led for so many years, through the Exodus and the forty years of wandering in the wilderness. Think of someone whom you can speak a blessing over, and then do it this week.

1 SAMUEL 2:1-10

The Lord gives both death and life; he brings
some down to the grave but raises others up.

– 1 Samuel 2:6

You sometimes wonder what I'm up to. You think maybe I am no longer in control when things don't turn out according to your plan. You wonder if I have stopped caring about you or listening to your prayers.

There is no reason to fear—I act out of my holiness. I know all things, and I weigh every action, so you can be sure that my ways are right. To question me is to speak from a place of pride. Choose instead to trust that my ways are best.

I bring down the mighty and give strength to the weak. The full go away empty, while the hungry are filled. The barren woman has seven children, and the mother of many children is forlorn. I raise the poor from the dust and make them sit with princes.

All of these surprises are part of my care for my faithful ones. I do what is just and right. So if you feel I have dealt harshly with you, take heart. All things are worked out in my time and my way, according to my perfect plan. Trust that I do everything well.

God accomplishes all his holy purposes. Have you been fighting against his decrees? Trust that he knows best and submit to him today.

July

1 SAMUEL 15:22-23

Obedience is better than sacrifice, and submission
is better than offering the fat of rams.

– 1 Samuel 15:22

I don't want your empty promises. You can't hide from me—I know your heart better than you know it yourself. I don't want your good deeds and sacrifices, I want obedience. A heart devoted to doing right. Submission to my will rather than insistence on going your own way.

If you will give me your heart, I will give you so much more. I will give you my heart. I will replace your stony, hard heart with a heart of flesh. I will give you my Spirit, who will remind you of everything I have told you and give you power to obey me. I will make you my own dear child. I will declare you beloved. Chosen. Forgiven. Redeemed.

I have given you all this; won't you give me your heart?

All our rituals of devotion are empty if they are not backed up by a life of obedience. As James said, faith without works is dead (James 2:17). Are you trying to earn God's favor through acts of piety without really giving him your heart in obedience? It won't work—God sees your heart, and he loves you so much that he wants it all for himself.

2 SAMUEL 22:1-16

*My God is my rock, in whom I find protection. He is my
shield, the power that saves me, and my place of safety.*

– 2 Samuel 22:3

Let me be your rock. Your fortress. Your deliverer. Find refuge in me, not in the temporary securities the world offers. For I am a shield and a horn of salvation to all who call on me.

When the waves of death overwhelm you, I am your helper. When torrents of destruction assail you, come to me. Call on me, for I will hear you. When the earth reels and rocks, when the very heavens tremble on their foundations, when the earth gives way beneath your feet, cry out to me.

I will bow the heavens to come and help you. I will ride on the wings of the wind to come to your aid. With a word, I will calm the storm, pull you out of the waters, and rescue you. I am your Savior, and I will keep you safe.

Meditate on the power of God that is described in these verses, and then think about the fact that all this power is unleashed on your behalf when you pray.

2 SAMUEL 22:17-29

He led me to a place of safety; he rescued me because he delights in me.
— 2 Samuel 22:20

My hand reaches down to save you. I pluck you out of danger and pull you out of the waters that threaten to drag you under. When people rise against you, I am your support.

Look at the place I have brought you to. It is wide open, full of delight and possibility. I brought you here because I delight in you. I want good things for you. I want to spend time with you.

To the merciful I show myself merciful, and the one who is humble I raise up. Do what is right, and I will light up the darkness around you.

Let me be your firm place to stand.

If you feel as though you're drowning today, trust that God is bringing you to a place of safety. He delights in you, and he will draw you out of the deep waters and place you on solid ground.

July
4

2 SAMUEL 22:30-51

God's way is perfect. All the LORD's promises prove true.
He is a shield for all who look to him for protection.

– 2 Samuel 22:31

You can do great things with me! You can run against an army. You can climb on the rocky high places as sure-footed as a deer. Nothing I give you to do is too difficult for you—just rely on my strength and you can do it.

I lead you with gentleness and tender care. My strong hand lifts you up and makes your feet secure. I show you each foothold as you climb to the heights. I am leading you up out of danger, to a place where you can be close to me and gain perspective on all I am doing.

All my ways are perfect, and every word I speak proves true. Trust me as I lead you, day by day, to new places. It will be worth the journey—just keep following me and you will see.

How would you live differently today if you truly believed that God is your shield and that all his ways are perfect? Turn your worries over to him and then live out your confidence that God is mightily working in your life to bring about his perfect plan.

July
5

1 KINGS 8:22-61

O LORD, God of Israel, there is no God like you in all of heaven above or on the earth below. You keep your covenant and show unfailing love to all who walk before you in wholehearted devotion.

– 1 Kings 8:23

What separates me from all the false gods is that I love you steadfastly, even when you rebel and forsake me. I sought you before you sought me. I saved you even though you didn't deserve it. I keep my promises even though you break all your vows to me. No one else can do all that or even desires to do that.

Behold, I have compassion on you. My ears are open to your pleas. Whenever you cry out to me, I listen. You are my dear child, and I love you.

When bad things happen to you—even if your suffering is a result of your own sin—even then I am with you. I will be merciful to you and draw you close to my heart. Every word I have promised will come true; not one of them will fail. I have promised to be with you always, and I will do it.

Solomon's prayer is a good model for us. He engaged his body in prayer (verse 22), he praised God for his character (verses 23-24), and then he prayed that God would fulfill his promises—in other words, he prayed Scripture (verses 25-26). What could you adapt from Solomon's example to strengthen your own prayer life?

July
6

1 CHRONICLES 16:8-18

*Search for the L*ORD *and for his strength; continually seek him.*
– 1 Chronicles 16:11

Today, with all of its busyness and trouble, pause to praise me. Tell others of my greatness—it will be an encouragement to you and to them. Sing about my wondrous works. Glory in my holy name, and let your heart rejoice because your refuge is in me.

Don't forget me. Seek my presence continually. Remind yourself of the miracles I have done and the judgments I have uttered. Remember who you are to me: Chosen. Loved. Valuable. Child of my covenant love. You may be of little account in the world's eyes, but in my eyes, you are precious. Live with confidence because your position before me is secure.

These verses tell us to search for God's strength by continually pursuing him. One of the ways we do that is by praising him, and another is by reminding ourselves of his faithfulness in the past. Today, when you're feeling weak or overwhelmed, turn to God rather than trying to fix the problem on your own.

1 CHRONICLES 16:19-36

Publish his glorious deeds among the nations.
Tell everyone about the amazing things he does.

– 1 Chronicles 16:24

As you wander, feeling lost, remember that your true home is with me. You are not alone—I am with you. And you are not lost—I am leading you.

Here is how you can get your bearings: Sing of my salvation. Declare my glory among the nations. Tell people about all I have done for you. Worship me in all my holy magnificence.

When you do this, you join in the praises of creation. The heavens are glad because I reign, the good and true King. The seas roar and the fields exult in my power and mercy. The trees sing for joy before me, for they know I am the righteous judge who will make all things right. If even the natural order worships me, so should you.

When you remember who I am, you will be bold to live for me. You will be filled with joy, for you will know you are mine and I care for you in each moment.

When you're struggling with doubt, telling others about God's love will strengthen your faith. Publish abroad the amazing things he has done, and see how he will write his love on your heart.

1 CHRONICLES 29:10-22

Yours, O Lord, is the greatness, the power, the glory, the victory, and the majesty. Everything in the heavens and on earth is yours, O Lord, and this is your kingdom. We adore you as the one who is over all things.

– 1 Chronicles 29:11

When you bless me, offering yourself and all you have to me, you may feel like the sacrifice is great. But really you are just giving back to me what is already mine. Everything comes from me—I made it all. You are but a mist, here for a moment, yet I have blessed you with abundance and poured out my love on you.

Your giving is a test: Do you know who I am? Do you trust me to take care of you? Will you return to me what I have given you?

So make your offerings to me with joy. See how I will respond to your gift by pouring even more blessing out on you. When you give to me, trust that I will open the storehouses of heaven to provide for all your needs.

King David reminded the Israelites of who God is—his greatness—and the people naturally responded by bringing their offerings to the Lord. Do your actions and words inspire others to praise God? How can you grow in this area?

July
9

2 CHRONICLES 6:14-42

Will God really live on earth among people? Why, even the highest
heavens cannot contain you. How much less this Temple I have built!

– 2 Chronicles 6:18

The highest heaven cannot contain me, yet I have chosen to dwell with you. I am the almighty Creator, yet I entered into my creation as a helpless baby to be with you.

What great love I have for you! I moved heaven and earth to be close to you. I bent low to experience your world with you so I could save you from your sin. I entered the muck and heartache of humanity so we could be together forever.

Won't you come and be with me? Enter deep into the relationship I have made available to you. Walk with me in the cool of the day. Delight in me as I delight in you.

It is unbelievable to think about—the holy Creator chooses to dwell with his sinful creatures! This amazing invitation to enter into eternal relationship with the God of the universe is freely offered to you. Choose to spend time in God's presence today, thanking him for the grace that enables you to do so.

2 CHRONICLES 7:12-22

*If my people who are called by my name will humble themselves
and pray and seek my face and turn from their wicked ways, I will
hear from heaven and will forgive their sins and restore their land.*

– 2 Chronicles 7:14

I have heard your prayer. You have felt my hand of discipline heavy on you. Yet even now, if you will humble yourself, pray, seek my face, and turn from your rebellion, then I will hear from heaven and forgive your sin and heal your land. Gather with my people and repent together. Weep over your sin, over all the ways you have fallen short of my glory and failed to live up to my holy standards.

It's never too late to turn back to me. Your sin is never too great to be forgiven. Even today you can be healed from the heartache. All you have to do is humbly acknowledge your wrongdoing and choose to do what is right.

Don't let today go by without repenting. A fresh start awaits you! Freedom and forgiveness will come the instant you confess.

The actions of a nation have consequences, just as the actions of individuals do. Pray this verse for yourself, humbling yourself and turning from your sin. Then pray for your leaders by name, that they will humble themselves before God.

July
11

EZRA 9:5-15

*O my God, I am utterly ashamed; I blush to lift up
my face to you. For our sins are piled higher than our
heads, and our guilt has reached to the heavens.*

– Ezra 9:6

See what kind of God I am. I listen to the prayers of my people. When you are so ashamed you can hardly speak, I hear you. Despite your great guilt and the mountain of wrongs you have done against me, I listen.

And I forgive. Even when you were wallowing in sin, far from me, I preserved and kept you. I never forsook you even when you enslaved yourself to addictions and behaviors you knew were not pleasing to me. Even when I disciplined you, it was far less than your sins deserved.

Rejoice now in my deliverance. Give thanks for my mercy. In my kindness I preserved you. Now respond to that great grace with gratitude and love.

Ezra's prayer of confession is a good prayer for us to model our own prayers after. Acknowledge your guilt for both private and corporate sins, and thank God that he does not punish us as our sins deserve. With him is abundant forgiveness.

July 12

JOB 38:1-18

Where were you when I laid the foundations
of the earth? Tell me, if you know so much.

– Job 38:4

D o you dare to question me? Surely you do so without thinking. Let me question you . . .

Where were you when I laid the earth's foundations and determined its measurements? Did you stretch the tape measure and set the mountains in place? Did you hear the morning stars sing together at the moment of creation? Did you set the boundaries of the sea or give birth to the clouds? Did you say to the waters, "Thus far shall you come, and no farther?" Do you tell the sun to rise each morning? Have you walked on the deep places of the sea? Can you comprehend the expanse of the earth?

Then surely you should not question whether I know what I am doing. Trust me, the Creator who knows all things. I love you, and I do all things well. That is all you need to know.

These words from God to Job put us in our place. Read them slowly, reminding yourself of God's power and your own smallness. Then bring your requests to God with these thoughts in your mind.

JOB 38:19-36

Do you know the laws of the universe?
Can you use them to regulate the earth?

– Job 38:33

Before you ask me your questions, let me ask you a few. Have you seen the sheds where I store the snow? Do you know where I keep the hail, reserving it for the day of trouble? Do you know where I keep the light, or where I scatter the east wind?

Who charts the course for the rivers and marks targets for the lightning? Who sends the rain or makes the grass sprout and grow? Who conceives the drops of dew and births the glaciers? Do you lead the stars by name and place them in the sky?

I do all this, and I place wisdom in the heart of humankind. If I can do all this, surely you can honor me as the source of all wisdom. Surely you can trust me and rest in my judgments.

These words from God to Job put us in our place. Read them slowly, reminding yourself of God's power and your own smallness. Then bring your requests to God with these thoughts in your mind.

JOB 39

Is it at your command that the eagle rises to the heights to make its nest?

– Job 39:27

I am Lord over all things. I watch the mountain goats give birth. I let the wild donkeys go free, then lead them to pasture and care for them.

The ox won't do work for you of its own accord; it cares nothing for you. The wild ostrich doesn't even care for its own young, and it certainly won't hide you under its wings.

But I, the one who tells the animals where to build their nests and where to find food—I care for you. I meet all your needs and hide you under my wings of love. I care this much for the animals, and you are of far more importance than they are. Won't you trust me? Even today, even for all that concerns you, trust me. I am the all-powerful Creator who loves you and cares for you.

The beautiful poetry of these verses encourages us to look at God's care for nature. If he is able to care for all these seemingly insignificant animals, will he not also care for us? Turn your worries over to God and trust that he will take care of you.

July 15

JOB 40:7-24

Brace yourself like a man, because I have some questions for you, and you must answer them.

– Job 40:7

I f you want to question my ways, stand up and do it. Dress for action and bring me your angry questions. Tell me the ways you think I have wronged you. I will not turn you away; I will answer you with my thundering voice.

Behold, I draw out the mightiest sea creatures with a fishhook. The great beasts are like tame pets in my hand. Who can stand up to me? Who can give me anything that isn't already mine? I can do all things, and no purpose of mine is ever thwarted.

When you come before me with your questions, you will see me as I am, infinite in power and endless in mercy and love. And just like a mist, your questions will dissolve in the face of my glory and goodness.

It is no small thing to question God's ways, but God patiently puts up with our doubts. If you're struggling in your faith, be honest with God about it. Don't be afraid to bring him your questions—just be sure you're prepared for his answers.

PROVERBS: MONEY MATTERS

*In the blink of an eye wealth disappears, for it
will sprout wings and fly away like an eagle.*

– Proverbs 23:5

Money is a tool; it can be used to help others and as a test for where your true treasure is. When you give generously, it shows that your heart trusts me to provide. How you spend your money reveals what is in your heart.

Don't fall for get-rich-quick schemes. I want you to work hard and receive the rewards of your labor. But the rewards I give are not always in the form of material blessing. If you are fed and clothed, that is enough. Be content; your true reward is in heaven.

Don't rely on your wealth to keep you secure. It can disappear in an instant, and it isn't really yours anyway—all you have comes from me. Choose instead to find your security in me and you will be building on a secure foundation.

Everything we have comes from God, and we are merely stewards of it. We should keep this in mind whenever we make decisions related to money. We must also remember that wealth doesn't last and is capable of turning our hearts away from God.

PROVERBS: WISDOM

Fear of the LORD is the foundation of wisdom.
Knowledge of the Holy One results in good judgment.

– Proverbs 9:10

Wisdom is better than rubies—it is of more value than anything else you desire. It will help you live well in any situation. So seek wisdom and humbly accept rebuke when you act foolishly. Apply your heart to instruction, seeking it out like the treasure it is.

I am the source of all wisdom. Reverence me in your heart, listen to my Word, and you will become wise. You will find the path of life and peace.

Do you need more convincing to seek wisdom? Think of all its benefits, both in this life and the next: favor, happiness, health, honor, and prosperity. Live according to my commandments and you will be wise.

Wisdom is the ability to live well, and the source of wisdom is God himself. If you seek God, studying the Bible to learn about him and his commandments, you will become wise.

July
18

PROVERBS: WORK

Good planning and hard work lead to prosperity,
but hasty shortcuts lead to poverty.

– P r o v e r b s   2 1 : 5

Only fools are lazy. They don't plan ahead, and in the end they are not prepared for the day of drought. Don't be like them, always resting and never working. One day poverty will overtake them.

Think of the ants, always working to prepare for winter. Likewise, the person who tends the fig tree gets to eat of its fruit. The one who works hard will be able to provide for their family.

There is great satisfaction in hard work. The virtuous person rises early and sometimes works into the night. He or she plants a vineyard and uses its profit to care for the needy. Enjoy the fruit of your hands and let your works praise you in the gates.

Satisfying work is a gift from God. Anything we do can be an act of worship, so work hard at the occupation God gives you. Even unskilled, tedious tasks can be done to his glory.

PROVERBS: PRIDE AND HUMILITY

Pride leads to disgrace, but with humility comes wisdom.

– P r o v e r b s   1 1 : 2

I hate pride, therefore I give grace to the lowly. Pride leads to shame, but humility leads to honor. Humility is the path to riches, honor, and life.

I am close to those who acknowledge their need of me and confess their sin. I draw near to those who honor me as God.

So don't lift yourself up; wait for others to honor you. Let someone else point out your successes. You know that I have said the last shall be first and the first shall be last. Follow my example of humble service to my disciples—that is the way of love.

In God's economy, the way to become great is to become a servant. The way to success is through humility. So be willing to take the low position, considering others as better than yourself and serving in the lowliest tasks, and wait for God to lift you up.

PROVERBS: WORDS

Gentle words are a tree of life; a deceitful tongue crushes the spirit.

– P r o v e r b s   1 5 : 4

Your mouth will utter the words your heart speaks. What you say is an overflow from your inner soul-life. Feed your heart well and you will speak well.

Fill yourself with my Word. Open your heart to receive my life and you will overflow with life-giving words. Fill your mind with wholesome and virtuous things and you will speak truth.

Don't speak thoughtlessly or rashly. Think carefully about whether your words will build up or tear down, and then only say things that are encouraging. Learn my ways of peace so you can build others up.

What do your words say about your heart? Proverbs instructs us to use kind, patient, gentle words rather than harsh or angry ones. Pay attention today to the kinds of words and the tone you use, and then talk with God about how to improve your speech Proverbs-style.

PROVERBS: FRIENDSHIP

Love prospers when a fault is forgiven,
but dwelling on it separates close friends.

– Proverbs 17:9

I am your true friend, the one who sticks closer than a brother. When you understand just how much I love you, you will overflow with love for your neighbors.

Watch that your habits of thought, speech, and action encourage true friendship. Practice loyalty and kindness. Be slow to get angry, and instead work for peace. Think the best of others so you don't get ruffled over little misunderstandings.

In times of need, be there for your friends. Listen to them, just as I listen to you. Help and support them, sharing their burdens even as I carry yours. True friendship helps others see my love—be that kind of friend.

Would your friends say you are a true friend to them? Think and pray about how you can be a better friend—one who helps in time of need, who forgives rather than holds a grudge, and who is loyal.

July 22

PROVERBS: FEAR OF THE LORD

Fear of the LORD leads to life, bringing security and protection from harm.
– **P r o v e r b s 1 9 : 2 3**

All of these proverbs are summarized in one sentence: Fear me and become wise. Revere and honor me in your heart, and you will know how to live well. Not only that, but you will desire to obey me because you will trust in my love.

Out of my mouth come knowledge and understanding. Those who walk in my ways will be secure—both in their relationship with me and in their relationships with others.

Trust me and lean on my understanding, and I will guide your path. Commit all your ways to me and you will succeed. Do what is right even when it is difficult and you will be blessed.

So many things become clear if we fear the Lord, approaching him with awe at who he is and humility at who we are. That is the basis for obeying him, serving him, and even loving him. Are there ways in which you need to grow your fear of the Lord? Have you been thinking of him only as your friend, forgetting that he is also your Creator and Lord?

ECCLESIASTES 1:1-10

Generations come and generations go, but the earth never changes.

– Ecclesiastes 1:4

The sun rises and sets. The wind blows and streams flow to the sea in an endless cycle. People come and go, moving on from one thing to another. There is nothing new under the sun. All your toiling can't change these realities. You live and die, and hopefully you leave your mark on the next generation.

But this life is not all there is! Your soul will live on. And because you have trusted in me for salvation, you have assurance that when you die, you will be with me forever.

So don't wallow in the endlessness of life. Don't let it cause you to despair, like those who don't know me. Instead, let it draw you toward what lasts into eternity: your relationship with me.

It's easy to become hopeless if you look only at this life, with all its troubles and toils. But if you look beyond, to the heavenly reward that awaits those who love the Lord, you can enjoy the pleasures of this life as a foretaste of the true pleasures in heaven.

July 24

ECCLESIASTES 2:1-11

*As I looked at everything I had worked so hard to
accomplish, it was all so meaningless—like chasing the
wind. There was nothing really worthwhile anywhere.*

– Ecclesiastes 2:11

The things of this world will always leave you wanting more. You can choose to pursue pleasure, possessions, and greatness, but they will leave you empty, and they don't last anyway.

All the good gifts of this life—eating and drinking, finding satisfaction in your work, and the pleasure of loving relationships—are designed to point you to me. They come from my hand and serve as foretastes of the deeper joy you can find only in me.

So let my good gifts be a source of joy to you. Enjoy them with me.

Don't try to replace your yearning for me with them, but instead fill yourself with me and then you can fully enjoy the life I've given you.

Do you find yourself spending your time and energy seeking after things that only hold value in this life, or are you pursuing things that last into eternity? Everything this world offers is designed to point to the greater realities of life with God; they are not an end in themselves.

ECCLESIASTES 3:1-8

For everything there is a season, a time for every activity under heaven.

– Ecclesiastes 3:1

There is a time for joy and a time for sorrow. A time for beginnings and a time for endings. A time to scatter and a time to gather. A time to search and a time to give up the search and move on. A time to tear and a time to mend. A time for words and a time for silence. A time for war and a time for peace.

The moments of your life pass by in an endless cycle of change, but through it all I am with you. The changes from birth to death, from weeping to laughter, are part of my design for life on earth.

So don't fret over the passage of time. I set the seasons of your life. Just when you think you can't take any more heartache, something changes and you're in a new season. Or just when you get too comfortable, things change to remind you to depend on me.

Let me show you what time it is—a time for planting or for harvesting, a time for mourning or for dancing. Allow me, the unchanging one, to lead and comfort you through each season of life.

It's easy to fret over the life we see slipping through our fingers— another birthday, another milestone, another season of life passes us by. But these seasons are part of the life God has made for us. Trust him to lead you through, and to help you find the joy and meaning in each stage.

July
26

ECCLESIASTES 3:9-22

*God has made everything beautiful for its own time. He has planted
eternity in the human heart, but even so, people cannot see the whole
scope of God's work from beginning to end. So I concluded there is
nothing better than to be happy and enjoy ourselves as long as we can.*

– Ecclesiastes 3:11-12

I know what is breaking your heart today. I see the awful injustice. I
see the brokenness and sorrow.

Take heart! The story isn't over. I make everything beautiful in its time.
I am working, even now, to restore what is broken and ugly. Whatever I
do endures forever, and nothing can be added to it or taken away from it.
I don't reveal my ways to you, because I want you to learn to wait on me
and trust me to work things out.

Trust me to turn the twisted and ugly things into something beautiful.
I am the Redeemer and healer. When I am finished, it will be even more
beautiful than it could have been without the brokenness. Wait and see
what I will do!

The writer of Ecclesiastes concludes that God's will for us on
earth is to accept our lot in life, be happy with the work God has
entrusted to us, and enjoy the gifts he gives. Trust him today with
your disappointments, and choose joy over despair.

ECCLESIASTES 4

*Two people are better off than one, for they can help each
other succeed. If one person falls, the other can reach out
and help. But someone who falls alone is in real trouble.*

– E c c l e s i a s t e s   4 : 9 - 1 0

Relationships are difficult—I know that because I lived through them too. People are unkind. They misunderstand one another. They act out of pride and selfishness. They hurt and betray you.

Even so, two are better than one. Life together is worth the difficulties, because you can help each other in times of need and comfort each other on cold, lonely nights.

But even better is a cord of three strands. Put me in the center of your relationships, and as you each grow closer to me, you will naturally grow closer to each other. When you allow me meet your needs, you will find yourself less needy and more able to give love to others. Let me enter in and see how strong your relationships can be.

The difficulties inherent in relationships can make us better people, rubbing off our rough places and helping us see our blind spots. But that can happen only if we submit to the process, inviting God to use our loved ones to help us grow. Are you willing to do that?

ECCLESIASTES 5:1-7

As you enter the house of God, keep your ears open and your mouth shut.
– Ecclesiastes 5:1

I love it when you seek my presence, when you come to my house or invite me into yours. When you draw near, come to listen. Don't fill all the silence with your own words. Instead, listen to my eternal words of truth.

When you make promises to me, be careful to keep them. It is better not to make a vow than to make one and not keep it.

That is why silence is so important. Words can easily lead you into sin or pride; waiting on me leads to humility, right thoughts, and careful actions. Sit before me in silence and let me speak to your heart. Then respond with careful words and thoughtful prayers.

When we pray, it's tempting to fill all the silences with words. But our silence is what allows God to speak to our hearts. In your prayer time today, try to sit silently before God with no agenda, no babbling— just to listen.

ECCLESIASTES 5:8-17

We all come to the end of our lives as naked and empty-handed
as on the day we were born. We can't take our riches with us.

– E c c l e s i a s t e s   5 : 1 5

D on't be surprised at the injustice of the world. People are only out for themselves. They take advantage of and oppress others to meet their own needs. They love money more than people. But even if these wicked people get rich from exploiting others, they will never be satisfied.

The ones who work an honest day's labor will sleep well. They will be satisfied with their toil and at peace with themselves and others.

It is good for you to find enjoyment in your work, and to enjoy the fruit of your labors with a grateful heart. If you live this way you will reach the end of your life and be satisfied with how you have lived.

Bumper stickers and memes tell us we can't take it with us—news Solomon first told us in Ecclesiastes. With that in mind, we should work for things that last. Who or what can you invest in today that will pay dividends into eternity?

ECCLESIASTES 7:1-10

A good reputation is more valuable than costly perfume.
And the day you die is better than the day you are born.

– Ecclesiastes 7:1

It is good to think soberly about life and death, to live with the end in mind. Mortal, earthly life is destined to end, so make sure you're living in such a way that you are investing in things that truly matter.

It is better to have a good reputation than a lot of money. It is better to be patient than proud, better to hold your anger in check than to let it loose. Live wisely today, honoring me with the way you conduct yourself, and you will have no regrets.

Content yourself with what I have given you. Don't pine away for the life you used to have, or the one you wish you had. You can't change what I have given you, so you might as well rejoice in what is rather than spoiling my good gifts wishing for something else.

What we value says a lot about who we are. Do you value a good reputation more than riches? The refining that comes through sorrow more than temporary pleasure? Think through your calendar and your bank account, and see if you truly value what you profess to value.

ECCLESIASTES 7:13-22

Accept the way God does things, for who can straighten what he has made crooked?
– Ecclesiastes 7:13

Some days are full of joy, and others are full of sorrow. Happy tears mingle with sad ones, and both come from my hand.

Life's uncertainties are designed to make you turn to me, the only one who can help you. When things are good and life is going well, sometimes you think you can get by fine without me. But when life gets difficult you realize how much you need me, how helpless you truly are.

On those hard days, lean in to me. Learn from me how to be at peace, regardless of circumstances. Let me show you how to find joy in the midst of pain. For I am in control of all things, and I am working all things for your good and my glory. Trust that in my hand, the happiness and the sorrow have a good purpose.

The apostle Paul said that true godliness with contentment is great wealth (1 Timothy 6:6). That is really the theme of this passage—contentment with where we are in life, with the joys and sorrows of today, with the circumstances God has chosen for us. But contentment comes through self-discipline. How can you foster contentment in your heart today?

August

ECCLESIASTES 12

That's the whole story. Here now is my final conclusion:
Fear God and obey his commands, for this is everyone's duty.

– Ecclesiastes 12:13

Turn to me in your youth, while you still have strength and years before you. Give yourself to me while you still find pleasure in life, before you are stooped and slow. Choose well how you will live when you are young so that you can give all your days to me. Then you will have many years to enjoy and serve me, and you will have the security of knowing that when you die, you will live in my presence forever.

Let words of wisdom and delight guide your life. Use my words of truth as goads to keep you on the right path, for all wisdom comes from me. Your whole duty is to fear me and keep my commandments. If you do this, you will live well and be at peace.

Solomon urges his readers to take hold of his conclusions about the meaning of life while they are young, thereby sparing themselves the searching process he went through in the book of Ecclesiastes. How would your life change if you lived by the wisdom found in this book?

August

2

SONG OF SONGS

Place me like a seal over your heart, like a seal on your arm.
For love is as strong as death, its jealousy as enduring as the
grave. Love flashes like fire, the brightest kind of flame.

– Song of Songs 8:6

I am your bridegroom, the lover of your soul. You are beautiful to me, truly delightful in my sight. When you were lost, I sought you and found you.

Arise and come away with me! The winter is past, and the rain is over and gone. Come sit in my shadow, for I am yours and you are mine. Enjoy the freedom of knowing how loved you are.

Set me as a seal on your heart, for love is as strong as death. I love you with a jealous love; I do not want to share you with lesser gods. Many waters cannot quench the love I have for you. It is a forever love, a consuming fire.

Scripture uses the analogy of marriage to illustrate the relationship between Christ and the church (see Ephesians 5). He loves us with that kind of fierce, jealous, seeking love. Spend time in his presence soaking up his love, meditating on the truth that God loves you that deeply.

ISAIAH 1:1-20

"Come now, let's settle this," says the LORD. *"Though your sins are like scarlet, I will make them as white as snow. Though they are red like crimson, I will make them as white as wool."*

– Isaiah 1:18

I loved you and cared for you and even died to save you—yet you have rebelled against me. You have put other things before me, making them into little idols in your heart. Even when you do repent, it isn't sincere. I don't want your sacrifices or your empty promises.

What I want is a clean heart. Wash yourself in my blood and you will be clean. Cease to do evil and learn to do good. Seek justice and correct oppression. These are the signs of a pure heart, of someone who is truly repentant.

Come, let us reason together. Though your sins have stained you red like scarlet, I can make you white as snow. No matter how dark the blot, I can purify you. Your sin will be completely removed, leaving no sign that it was ever there. Turn to me in obedience and I will do this for you!

Isaiah's prophecy here is harsh. These things are true of us, too, and as we read these words it should drive us to our knees in repentance. But don't miss the precious words of verse 18. God forgives. No matter what we have done, he will forgive, cleanse, and purify us. Let him do that for you today.

August
4

ISAIAH 2

The LORD will mediate between nations and will settle
international disputes. They will hammer their swords into
plowshares and their spears into pruning hooks. Nation will
no longer fight against nation, nor train for war anymore.

– Isaiah 2:4

There will come a day when I will be lifted up and worshiped throughout the earth. People will stream into churches and seek me. In that day the proud will be brought low. People will cast away their idols and hide from my judgment. The haughtiness of people's hearts will be humbled, and they will worship me alone.

But you can come before me in humble worship even now, for you know me already. When you humble yourself before me, I will lift you up. You will not face judgment, for you are already declared righteous in my sight through my blood. I have forgiven you and made peace between us.

How we long for the day of peace described here, when the Lord mediates between nations and warfare ceases. As we look forward to that day, let us practice peace with our neighbors and work for the spread of the gospel worldwide.

ISAIAH 5

My beloved had a vineyard on a rich and fertile hill. He plowed the land, cleared its stones, and planted it with the best vines. In the middle he built a watchtower and carved a winepress in the nearby rocks.

– Isaiah 5:1-2

See what I have done for my beloved people. I have tended you like a vineyard. I cleared the stones from your heart. I planted vines and built a watchtower. I protected you and loved you.

Yet you grew wild grapes, settling for less than my best. You did not love me with your whole heart, and you chose to worship other things. So I will remove the hedge I built to protect you. I will deal justly and righteously with you.

Do you want to turn this situation around? I am the true vine; abide in me and you will find life. I am the gardener; submit to my pruning and you will bear fruit. Let me bring life from your barren branches as you remain in me and allow my Word to remain in you. It's not too late—turn back to me and you will once again live a fruitful life in my love and protection.

God performs the tasks described in these verses for everyone who loves him (see also John 15). Think about how he has tended you, protected you, loved you, and pruned you. Have you submitted to the processes that will lead to spiritual growth, or are you trying to fight against God's work in your life?

August
6

ISAIAH 8:11-17

Make the Lord of Heaven's Armies holy in your life.
He is the one you should fear. He is the one who should
make you tremble. He will keep you safe.

– Isaiah 8:13-14

People worry about world events or the fate of their job. They fear the death of a loved one or the end of an era. You should not fear what they fear, for dread has no place in your heart and mind if you trust in me.

Regard me as holy and revere me in your heart. As long as you worship and serve me with your life, you will have nothing to fear, for you will be in the center of my will.

When things are hard, believe me even then. I will protect and provide for you no matter what. Consider how I care for the lilies of the field and the birds of the air. If I care for them, surely you can trust me to meet all your needs—physical and spiritual. Do not fear, for I will provide.

Whom or what do you fear? What keeps you up at night? Build your life around the fear of the Lord and you won't need to fear anything in this life or the life to come.

ISAIAH 9:1-7

The people who walk in darkness will see a great light.
For those who live in a land of deep darkness, a light will shine.

– Isaiah 9:2

Before I came, all was darkness. Then I crashed into time and space. I entered the world I created and took on human flesh to bring light for all who walk in darkness. I broke the yoke of sin and evil that enslaved you. I am your Wonderful Counselor, Mighty God, Everlasting Father, Prince of Peace.

My peace is everlasting. Through me, you have a joyous relationship with God almighty. And there will be justice and peace forever because of what I have done—justice for all the evil in the world and peace in your inmost being as you live with me in blessed communion.

Do you live in the light, believing these truths? Or do you still stumble in the dark through disbelief? Come into the light!

The light of Jesus shines in every dark corner of the world, dispelling the gloom with the light of his truth and righteousness. Think of the pockets of darkness you see around you, and pray that he will bring the light of his presence into those places and situations.

ISAIAH 11:1-10

Out of the stump of David's family will grow a shoot—
yes, a new Branch bearing fruit from the old root.

– Isaiah 11:1

I bring life out of death. The stump of Jesse—lifeless, cut down, without hope or purpose—sprouted new life. From it came Messiah. Son of God. Bringer of life. I broke into this dead world, full of dead people walking in the death of sin, and I shattered death.

I, the Lord, decide not by what I see or hear, but with righteousness. Everything I do is right and holy. When all my purposes are accomplished and I return to rule in the new heaven and the new earth, you will see the wolf dwelling with the lamb, the calf and the lion living together, and everything at peace. There will be no more death or destruction, for the earth will be full of the knowledge of me as the waters cover the sea.

So don't think that just because something looks like a dead end, it is.

I bring life from death and peace from strife, and my resting place is glorious.

Make a list of all God's attributes described in these verses, and all the promises that are made about the Kingdom of God. Let these truths encourage you today.

ISAIAH 12

God has come to save me. I will trust in him and not be afraid.
The Lord God is my strength and my song; he has given me victory.

— Isaiah 12:2

I came to save you. Trust me and do not be afraid. When you are hopeless, my strength will comfort you and give you a song to sing.

Come, drink deeply from the well of salvation. It is life, and it will never run dry. Let me fill the dried-up well of your soul with living water. Drink of me and you will never thirst again, for you will have the waters of salvation welling up within you.

Give me thanks and call on my name. Make my wonderful deeds known among the nations. Sing praise for all I have done for you. I, the Holy One of Israel, am in your midst.

This is a victory song. Think of the areas in your life where God has brought victory. Now pray for those areas where you long for victory, and claim his promise that he is your strength and your song.

August 10

ISAIAH 14:1-3

But the LORD will have mercy on the descendants of Jacob. He will choose Israel as his special people once again. He will bring them back to settle once again in their own land. And people from many different nations will come and join them there and unite with the people of Israel.

– Isaiah 14:1

When I look at you, even on days when you've made a mess of things, I am filled with compassion. Each day, each moment, I choose you. No matter how unlovely you feel, I love you and choose you to be my beloved.

I am making for you a special place in heaven. One day I will bring you there, and you will dwell with me forever. There you will have rest from all the turmoil of your sojourn on earth.

Reject the labels people try to give you and the lies they try to make you believe about who you are. Live this day as my beloved, as someone who is chosen, as someone who has a home being prepared for them in heaven. For this is your true identity.

The word used here for *mercy* represents a mother's care for her child. Meditate on the truth that God cares for you as a mother cares for her beloved child, with a tender touch and compassionate concern for all your needs.

ISAIAH 25

*He will swallow up death forever! The Sovereign LORD will
wipe away all tears. He will remove forever all insults and
mockery against his land and people. The LORD has spoken!*

– Isaiah 25:8

I am your stronghold in the day of distress, a shelter from the storm and a shade from the heat. My promises are your hope and shield.

On my mountain I will lay out a feast for all my people, those from every nation on earth who love me. The veil will be removed so you can see me face-to-face. All tears will be wiped away, every reproach will be removed, and we will feast together on well-aged wine and rich food. What a day that will be!

And it is all because of the Cross, that plan formed of old. I swallowed up death forever and removed the curse of sin. You waited for me, and I saved you. Rejoice in this wonderful salvation and in the hope of that great marriage supper of the Lamb at the end of time.

Which of these promises do you need to hear today? Read the passage slowly, and then write down the verse that stands out to you. Keep it in a place where you can reread it and meditate on it throughout the day.

August 12

ISAIAH 26

Lord, you will grant us peace; all we have accomplished is really from you.

– Isaiah 26:12

A stable heart is one that has truth written on its walls and bulwarks. Peace comes through keeping your mind fixed on me and arming yourself with my promises. Trust me, for I am your rock.

I see that you yearn for justice, begging me to fix everything that is wrong in the world. Here is truth: Justice is coming. Wait on me, for I will deal with sin and strike down those who do evil. I am coming from my throne in righteousness to uncover sin and punish iniquity.

Don't fear what you see going on around you—I have already won. On that day when I return, the dead in Christ will live. They will rise up and sing for joy! My life-giving light will fall over the earth as dew. Fix your heart on this certain hope and be at peace.

Every promise God has made is so sure it's as if it has already been fulfilled. Many Bible writers emphasized this truth by writing of future events in the past tense. Today, as you cope with difficulties and fears, cling to God's promises with the knowledge that they are certain.

August
13

ISAIAH 29:13-24

He is the Potter, and he is certainly greater than you, the clay!
Should the created thing say of the one who made it, "He didn't
make me"? Does a jar ever say, "The potter who made me is stupid"?

– Isaiah 29:16

I am the potter, and you are the clay. I made you, and therefore I understand you better than you understand yourself. I know when your worship is sincere, and when your heart is far from me. So don't try to hide from me, and don't question my ways.

In a little while, I will return and set everything right. Deaf people will hear, and the blind will see. The meek will obtain fresh joy in me. The poor will exult in me.

In that day you will no longer be ashamed or afraid. You will stand in awe of me, your Savior, and be amazed at the blessings I have poured out on you. You will see my holiness, and in that moment you will understand everything that has come before. Live today in the shadow of that day, embracing the reality that all my promises are true.

This passage is about pride—the pride of worshiping God according to our preferences rather than his commands, the pride of thinking we know better than God, and the pride of sin. By contrast, the humble will be filled with fresh joy from the Lord (verse 19). Take these words seriously; repent of your pride and foster humility in your heart.

August 14

ISAIAH 30

*This is what the Sovereign L*ORD*, the Holy One of Israel, says:*
"Only in returning to me and resting in me will you
be saved. In quietness and confidence is your strength."

– Isaiah 30:15

A h, stubborn children, always trying to go your own way and unwilling to hear my instruction—turn to me before it's too late!

In returning and rest you will be saved. Be quiet and trust my work of salvation. Don't try to make up your own way to be saved, adding to what I have commanded or lessening my requirements. I have saved you— don't try to add to what I have already done. You will find strength in quietness and trust, not in striving and pride.

I wait to be gracious to you; I love to lavish mercy on you. Happy are those who wait for me, who trust in me alone for salvation. They will find joy instead of sadness, for they will see me as I am and I will give them a song to sing.

Judah had doubted God's power and made an alliance with Egypt even though God had told them not to. They were trusting in the power of humans rather than the power of God. But the truth is, for them as well as for us, true power comes from resting in God and letting him fight our battles.

ISAIAH 31-32

*This righteousness will bring peace. Yes,
it will bring quietness and confidence forever.*

– I s a i a h   3 2 : 1 7

Bad things are coming for those who place their trust in powerful people instead of in me. They think they can trust what they see—strong leaders with large armies—but forget to look to me, the Holy One.

I am the all-powerful warrior-King. On that day when I come down to fight evil and injustice, there will be terror in the land for those who work evil. In that day all people will know that I am the Lord, more powerful than any other, and they will bow before me.

I am the one who brings true life. When I pour out my Spirit, the wilderness becomes a fruitful field and the fruitful field becomes a forest. Justice and righteousness rule over the land, and there is peace. Trust in me, believing these promises, and you will live in quiet confidence. You have a secure dwelling in me, and I will bring you to quiet resting places.

When we choose to trust in our own power rather than the power of God, we will be defeated. But when we humbly admit our weakness, God shows up. He replaces our weakness with his strength and gives us quiet confidence as we trust in him.

ISAIAH 33

The LORD will be our Mighty One. He will be like a wide river of protection that no enemy can cross, that no enemy ship can sail upon.

– Isaiah 33:21

As you wait on me, you will receive grace. I will be your strength each morning and your salvation in times of trouble.

I am exalted on high, for I fill the earth with justice and righteousness. I am your firm foundation in troubled times, stability when your world is reeling. With me is abundant salvation, wisdom, and knowledge—treasures beyond imagining. Each day I provide everything you need.

Come and dwell with me in the heights, in my fortress. There your eyes will behold me in my beauty. Come to this place of broad rivers and streams, the place of my majesty. Here you are safe and protected and loved.

The Assyrians were a wicked people with a mighty army. In human terms, Israel didn't stand a chance against them. But God was on their side, so victory was assured. What battles do you need to trust God for today?

ISAIAH 35

Say to those with fearful hearts, "Be strong, and do not fear, for your
God is coming to destroy your enemies. He is coming to save you."

– Isaiah 35:4

When you gaze on my glory and majesty, your joy and strength will blossom like a wilderness bursting to life and becoming a lush garden. The hardened ground of your soul will become a place of fruitfulness as you allow me to refresh you with my living water.

Strengthen your weak hands and make your shaking knees be still. Say to your anxious heart, "Be strong! Fear not! Behold, God is coming to save you!" I open the eyes of the blind and cause the deaf to hear. Those who were lame begin to leap for joy, and those who could not speak now sing happy songs.

You shall enter the gates of heaven with all my ransomed sinners, singing as you go. Everlasting joy will be upon your head, and you will have joy and gladness, for all sorrow shall flee. Encourage your heart with the assurance that these things will come to pass.

Who in your life is discouraged? Remind them of the promise in Isaiah 35:4. Meditate on the beautiful images of restoration and hope that are found in Isaiah 35, and pray that they will be true for yourself and for the people in your life who need refreshment.

August 18

ISAIAH 37

*Have you not heard? I decided this long ago. Long ago
I planned it, and now I am making it happen.*

– Isaiah 37:26

Did you receive bad news today? Is the future uncertain and frightening?

This is what I say to you: Do not be afraid. I can do all things. Even these circumstances are under my control, for I alone am God, the one who made heaven and earth. Nothing takes me by surprise, for I know all things. What I determined long ago will come to pass. Even the things you face today, which seem so out of control, are in my eternal will.

Trust me and see what I will do. You have nothing to fear, for I am your God. Strengthen your heart by repeating these promises to yourself; they are your lifeline. Anchor your soul in the truth that I am God, and I am good.

Hezekiah had a big problem, and his immediate response was to go to the Lord in prayer. What is your immediate response to bad news? Take your concerns to God and trust him to work everything according to his perfect will, for his glory and your good.

ISAIAH 40:1-26

*He will feed his flock like a shepherd. He will carry
the lambs in his arms, holding them close to his heart.
He will gently lead the mother sheep with their young.*

– Isaiah 40:11

Comfort one another with the good news—I have come! My glory has been revealed, and my Word stands forever.

I came in might, to conquer sin and rule in your heart. And I came with tenderness, gathering you in my arms like a good shepherd gathers his lambs. I have gently led you each day of your life.

I have measured the waters in the palm of my hand and weighed the mountains on my scales. I understand all things and rule over all nations. Look at the stars—I call them all by name and make sure not one is missing. I am the one who sits above the circle of the earth and stretches out the heavens like a tent. Surely you can trust me, your Savior and Shepherd, to take care of you today and always.

Let these words of comfort wash over you. Jesus has come, and he is coming again. He feeds his flock and carries them close to his heart. All the troubles that loom so large in the world and in your life are, in the light of his greatness, as tiny and insignificant as a grain of sand.

August
20

ISAIAH 40:28-31

But those who trust in the LORD will find new strength.
They will soar high on wings like eagles. They will run
and not grow weary. They will walk and not faint.

— I s a i a h   4 0 : 3 1

I am the everlasting God, the creator of the ends of the earth. I do not faint or get tired, and my understanding is unsearchable.

When you are fainting with exhaustion, I give you power to take the next step. When you have no strength left, I give you my might. Even young people faint and get weary. They fall down exhausted, unable to take even one more step.

But if you wait on me, I will renew your strength. You will rise up with wings like an eagle. You will run without getting tired. You will walk and never grow weary. You will be able to courageously run the race of life in my power instead of your own.

We can read these verses every morning and never tire of them. Trust in this truth: God will give you all the strength you need for today, and tomorrow he will do it again.

ISAIAH 41:1-20

Don't be afraid, for I am with you. Don't be discouraged,
for I am your God. I will strengthen you and help you.
I will hold you up with my victorious right hand.

– I s a i a h   4 1 : 1 0

I am the first and the last, the beginning and the end. The entire earth trembles before my wisdom and power.

Yet I chose you, calling you from the ends of the earth and its farthest corners. I made you my servant and my own child, and I will not cast you away, despite your sins.

Fear not, for I am with you. Do not be dismayed or discouraged, for I am your God and I am here to help you. I will be your strength when you are weak. I am your Redeemer, the Holy One of Israel, and I will hold you up with my righteous right hand. In me you can rejoice, for I make the wilderness a pool of water and the dry land springs of water.

This chapter gives us perspective on the events going on around us. God is the one who is in control—of world events and of our lives. That is why we do not need to fear; our loving and good and just heavenly Father holds everything in his capable hands. Fear not.

August
22

ISAIAH 42:1-9

I, the LORD, have called you to demonstrate my righteousness.

– Isaiah 42:6

I never grow tired of helping you. I treasure your faint spark of faith, and I will breathe life into it until it becomes a vibrant flame. I will be faithful to complete the work I have begun in you.

I stretched out the heavens and formed the earth. I give life and breath to all people. I am the Lord, and I created you and called you in righteousness.

I made you for a purpose—to be a light to the nations. Be my hands and feet as I open the eyes of the blind and break the chains of those who are imprisoned in guilt and shame. Spread my fame and my glory so that others may know me. I am the Lord, and I am doing a new thing in your heart and through your life.

God's ultimate purpose in everything he does is to bring glory to his name. One day every knee will bow before him and every tongue will confess that he is Lord. Think about the goals you have. Do they fit in with God's ultimate purpose? Do you need to rethink some of your priorities?

August
23

ISAIAH 42:10-17; 43:18-19

I am about to do something new. See, I have already begun!
Do you not see it? I will make a pathway through the
wilderness. I will create rivers in the dry wasteland.

– Isaiah 43:19

Sing to me a new song, for each day I do new things for you. Praise me from the ends of the earth, for I do all things perfectly. I go forth in might to reveal my glory in your heart and to the nations.

In these days I am patient, showing mercy and waiting for people to turn to me. But soon I will judge the earth. Evil will be punished and justice will be done.

As I spread my glory throughout the earth, I will lead you in a way you haven't known before, on new paths in uncharted territory. Don't worry, I will show you the way. I will turn the darkness in front of you into light and make the rough places level before your feet. I will make a pathway through the wilderness and rivers in the wasteland so you can be refreshed.

What areas of your life do you need God to refresh and bring new life to? Where do you need a pathway through the wilderness? Ask him to do it, and then look for him to act.

August
24

ISAIAH 43:1-17

I have ransomed you. I have called you by name; you are mine. When you go through deep waters, I will be with you. When you go through rivers of difficulty, you will not drown. When you walk through the fire of oppression, you will not be burned up; the flames will not consume you.

– Isaiah 43:1-2

You don't need to be afraid of anything, because I have redeemed you. I have called you by name and ransomed your soul. You are mine.

When you go through rivers of difficulty, I will be with you. The floodwaters may rise, but they will not overwhelm you. I may call you to walk through fire, but I will keep you from being burned. For I am the Holy One of Israel, and I am your Savior.

You are precious and honored in my eyes, and I love you. If someone tries to snatch you away, I will come rescue you. Even when you try to run away, I will chase after you and bring you home because I love you. There is no power that can snatch you out of my hand. You are safe and secure in my love.

Write out these verses and post them in a place where you will see them often in the week ahead. Live each day with the assurance that you are safe in God's care.

August
25

ISAIAH 44:1-8, 21-24

I, the LORD, *made you, and I will not forget you.*

– Isaiah 44:21

Don't be despondent over the destruction you see in the world and even in your own life. Let me pour out my Spirit into your thirsty soul. I will cause streams of living water to flow out of you, spilling onto the dry ground around you. Even your descendants will enjoy my blessing through you.

I can do this because I am the first and the last, the only true God. I see the end from the beginning. When I make a promise, I fulfill it. I am your Rock and your Redeemer.

So sing and rejoice even as you sit in the ash heap, for I have done wondrous things in your life and will keep on doing them. I have swept away your sins like a cloud. I formed you in the womb and redeemed you, and I will not forget you. I paid to set you free, and I will never abandon you.

Do you feel forgotten today? Like no one understands you, and no one cares about you? God does. He is your Creator and Redeemer, and he will not forget you. He paid the price to set you free, and he will never abandon you.

ISAIAH 45:1-13

I am the LORD; there is no other God. I have equipped you for battle.

– Isaiah 45:5

This big, intimidating task before you is one I have chosen for you. Don't fear it—I will go before you and level the path so you do not stumble. I will break down the gates and remove every obstacle. Step by step, I will reveal to you all you need to know in order to accomplish the work I have for you.

Then you will know I am God, and I love you. I called you by name even before you knew me. I prepared you for this work before you were born.

I am the Lord, the righteous and wise King, and there is no other. Don't fight against my plans for you. I made you, I know you, I love you—and I have called you to this work. Trust me, you were made for it and you can do it with my help.

So many times we are tempted to doubt God's judgment: Why did he make me with this weakness? Why can't I be good at that? Dear one, God made you just as you are with a purpose. You can do everything he calls you to do with the gifts and strength he provides.

ISAIAH 46

I have cared for you since you were born. Yes, I carried you before you were born. I will be your God throughout your lifetime—until your hair is white with age. I made you, and I will care for you.

– Isaiah 46:3-4

Before you were even born, while you were in your mother's womb, I carried you. And into your old age, I will still carry you. I made you, and I will lift you up and save you throughout your lifetime.

Remind yourself of all the times I have shown you that I alone am God. I declare the end from the beginning, and from ancient times things not yet done. My counsel will stand, and I will accomplish all my purposes. I have spoken, and it shall be.

So follow me. I know all things, I do all things, and I am working all things for your good because I love you. Trust me and walk in my ways, and all shall be well.

Do you believe these promises, that God has been with you since the day you were born and will be with you until the day of your death? Even if terrible things have happened to you, God was with you in those moments of pain. Think back over your life and thank him for being with you each moment.

ISAIAH 48

*This is what the LORD says—your Redeemer, the Holy One
of Israel: "I am the LORD your God, who teaches you what is
good for you and leads you along the paths you should follow."*

– Isaiah 48:17

I will be glorified in all things, even in the trials and difficulties of your life. I refine you with fire to purify you and forge you in the furnace of affliction to bring glory to my name. All of your troubles serve a purpose in your life.

I alone am God, the first and the last. I laid the foundations of the earth and spread out the heavens. Every part of creation came into being at the sound of my voice, and even now I am speaking and ordering the world. Draw near to me, and I will show you how I have worked my purposes throughout the generations.

I am the Lord who leads you on good paths. Pay attention to my commandments and your peace will flow like a river. You will not thirst when I lead you through the desert, for I will make water gush out of the rocks for you.

God knows the future, and nothing happens outside of his will. The good times and the bad times all come from his hand, and they all work together for a single purpose: so that we will live for him and experience the peace that comes only through knowing him.

ISAIAH 49

Can a mother forget her nursing child? Can she feel no love for the child she has borne? But even if that were possible, I would not forget you! See, I have written your name on the palms of my hands.

– Isaiah 49:15-16

I lovingly formed you in your mother's womb and named you as my own. I created you with a purpose: to call others into my light and show them how they can be satisfied in me.

I will never forget you or leave you alone. Can a mother forget her nursing child? Of course not—her body won't let her! Yet even if she could, I will never forget you. I have engraved you on the palms of my hands. Your needs are continually on my mind and close to my heart.

I will take care of you, and when others will see the way I love you and tend to your needs, they will turn to me. I will bless you in such a way that you won't even be able to contain all the good I pour out on you, for I am your Redeemer, the Mighty One.

The first half of this chapter (verses 1-13) is about the hope we have through Jesus. The second half is God's response to the Israelites' doubts that these promises would come to pass. If you're doubting God's promises today, take to heart these words of comfort. God will never forget you, and one day your life will proclaim the truth that God is your Redeemer.

August

30

ISAIAH 51:1-16

Those who have been ransomed by the LORD will return. They will enter Jerusalem singing, crowned with everlasting joy. Sorrow and mourning will disappear, and they will be filled with joy and gladness.

– Isaiah 51:11

When you seek me, you will experience my comfort in all your places of need and want. I bring refreshment to the dry places within you, causing your soul to flower like a lush garden. You will be glad and sing for joy. Your mourning will be turned to dancing.

Comfort yourself with the certain hope of your eternal future. The earth will wear out like an old shirt, but my salvation is forever. You don't need to fear what humans can do to you, for they wither like the grass and fade away.

I am the Lord. I stretched out the heavens and stir up the seas—everything happens at my command. When all is completed, you will come to my heavenly city with singing. Everlasting joy will be on your head, for sorrow and sighing will be no more.

Ultimately the promise of this verse is the hope of heaven, where there will be no more death or sorrow or pain or tears (see Revelation 21:4). As you encounter sorrows today, cling to this hope and share it with others.

ISAIAH 52

*Let the ruins of Jerusalem break into joyful song, for the L*ORD
*has comforted his people. He has redeemed Jerusalem. The L*ORD
has demonstrated his holy power before the eyes of all the nations.
All the ends of the earth will see the victory of our God.

– Isaiah 52:9-10

Wake up! Rise up from the dust of shame and disappointment and dress yourself in garments of salvation. Live out the reality that in me you have victory over sin and death. Make known this good news: I reign.

When you look at all I have done, it should make you burst into song. I have comforted you. I have redeemed you. I have bared my arm for all people to see my salvation. I have gone before you and been your rear guard. I have suffered and died and been raised again to rule in glory—all for you.

Be astonished at this great love I have for you, and let it move you to live for the praise of my glory.

God's redemption leaves people speechless (verse 15). Think of the things that weigh heavily on your heart today, and ask God to work so mightily in those situations that everyone stands in awe of him.

September

ISAIAH 53

*It was our weaknesses he carried; it was our sorrows that weighed him down.
And we thought his troubles were a punishment from God, a punishment for
his own sins! But he was pierced for our rebellion, crushed for our sins. He
was beaten so we could be whole. He was whipped so we could be healed.*

– Isaiah 53:4-5

I bore your griefs and carried every one of your sorrows. I was afflicted
for you. I was wounded for your transgressions and crushed for your
iniquities. The punishment you deserved was placed on me, the holy and
innocent one.

This was the Father's will—to crush the Son to make the offering for
sin. I was poured out, utterly spent in suffering, and it was all for you.

What great cost there was to ransom your soul from sin and death. I
spent all to pay for what you could not afford. But what great victory! The
worst thing that ever happened was the best thing that ever happened,
because it was by my stripes that you are healed. Healed from sin. Healed
from sickness. Healed from death. This is life indeed.

Spend time today meditating on the magnitude of Christ's
sacrifice for you and the great cost of your healing.

ISAIAH 54

Your Creator will be your husband; the LORD of Heaven's Armies is his name! He is your Redeemer, the Holy One of Israel, the God of all the earth.

— Isaiah 54:5

I am expanding my family. The tent of my people needs to be spread out to make room for more. Stretch it out! Move the stakes to the left and the right. See my great compassion for all people—even for you.

The mountains may fall, but my compassionate, everlasting love will never depart from you. The Lord of Heaven's Armies is your Redeemer and your Creator. I have called you back from grief and shame and disgrace, and my covenant of peace rests on you forever.

O afflicted one, storm-tossed and not comforted, let me be your eternal foundation. Turn to me, that you and your children may be established in righteousness. Trust in me, and you will be safe forever. This is your heritage.

These promises are fulfilled in the Kingdom of God and the church. Which of these promises have you seen fulfilled in the Christian church today? Which are ones you want to pray that you will see more of?

ISAIAH 55:1-7

Is anyone thirsty? Come and drink—even if you have no money!
Come, take your choice of wine or milk—it's all free!

– Isaiah 55:1

Are you thirsty? Come to the living water. Are you broke, with no hope of being able to purchase what you need? Eat and drink your fill. Are you empty? Come to me, the source of all life. Don't waste your resources on things that cannot satisfy. Delight yourself in me and you will find rich, deep life.

I am near to you, and I offer you my steadfast, sure love. Hear my words and receive the life they offer. My covenant of love and faithfulness is forever. Seek me, and I will pour out my Spirit on you and abundantly pardon you. It's not about what you have to offer me; it's about the wealth of blessing that I offer to you. Receive my generosity with joy.

These verses describe the salvation God offers. It is free, available for anyone, satisfying, and eternal. But this wonderful offer demands a response—turning from sin and to God for forgiveness (verses 6-7). Have you sought God for this great salvation?

ISAIAH 55:8-13

Just as the heavens are higher than the earth, so my ways are higher than your ways and my thoughts higher than your thoughts.

– Isaiah 55:9

It is human nature to think you know best. But if I am truly God, maker of all things, who with my power can do anything—it only makes sense that my ways are better than yours. Why do you question my decisions and doubt my goodness?

My thoughts are as much higher than yours as the heavens are above the earth. There isn't even a comparison! My ways are far above what you could even imagine. And I accomplish all my purposes—always. I am making for myself a name, revealing my holiness and love to all people.

Trust my ways and my character. Believe that I will bring you out of every difficulty to a place of eternal joy. Trust me and be at peace.

When you wonder what God is up to, why he's sending such hard things into your life, read these verses to be reminded that he is the mighty Creator, and his ways are much better and wiser than anything you can dream up. Are you willing to trust that he knows best, and that in the end you will see his power and love?

September

5

ISAIAH 56:1-8

I will bring them to my holy mountain of Jerusalem and will fill them with joy in my house of prayer. I will accept their burnt offerings and sacrifices, because my Temple will be called a house of prayer for all nations.

– Isaiah 56:7

You have big dreams. You have so many ideas of how you'd like things to be and of what you'd like to accomplish. And then you look at yourself and your situation, and you despair. It looks as though your dreams can never come true.

Take heart. All your dreams that I've planted in you—the precious things that are part of my plan for you—every one will come true. For they depend not on you, but on my limitless power.

I will give you a place within my Kingdom to fulfill all the dreams I've given you, and it will be even better than you imagine. My ways are mysterious and wonderful. Trust me, follow me, and watch all my promises come true.

It's easy to look at ourselves and focus on all our limitations. The eunuch truly was a "dried-up tree with no children and no future." But God will fulfill all our God-planted desires according to his plans, and his ways are always better than ours. Hang on to your dreams, pray about them, and see how God uses your life for his glory.

September

6

ISAIAH 58

This is the kind of fasting I want: . . . Let the oppressed go free,
and remove the chains that bind people. Share your food with the
hungry, and give shelter to the homeless. Give clothes to those who
need them, and do not hide from relatives who need your help.

– Isaiah 58:6-7

You can't "fake it" with me. I know whether or not your repentance is sincere. You can fool people around you by doing pious acts, but I know whether or not your heart is in it. I don't want your fasting or your empty words, I want your heart.

Here is sincere repentance: to loosen the bonds of evil, to free the oppressed, to generously share what you have with others, to help those in need.

When you do these things, I will make your light break forth. I will answer your prayers. I will satisfy your desires in scorched places. You will be like a well-watered garden, lush and fruitful, because you will be spending your life for my purposes rather than your own.

Sometimes we use our acts of piety to hide what's going on inside us. We talk about our prayer times in reverent tones, but then we're irritable with our spouses or roommates. We spend every evening out with friends but can't make time to serve with the homeless ministry. God is not fooled. He wants our hearts, and we'll know that he has them when we willingly serve those around us.

ISAIAH 59

*The Redeemer will come to Jerusalem to buy back those in Israel who
have turned from their sins," says the Lord. "And this is my covenant
with them . . . My Spirit will not leave them, and neither will these words
I have given you. They will be on your lips and on the lips of your
children and your children's children forever. I, the Lord, have spoken!*

– Isaiah 59:20-21

My hand is not shortened, as if I cannot save you. My ear is not
dull, as if I am unable to hear. The problem between us is your
sin. You've built up a wall with your rebellion against me, piling up your
wrongdoing so high you can't see me or hear me anymore. You grope
around in the dark because the walls you've built prevent my light from
coming through.

All you need to do to break through that wall is repent. Turn back
to me. Call your sin what it is—rebellion against your Creator and
Redeemer. Seek me, and I will break down the wall and save you the
moment you ask. Don't live in darkness anymore; let me come in and
forgive and heal.

If you're feeling as though a wall exists between you and God,
use this passage to confess your sins before him. Acknowledge
the ways you've separated yourself from him. And then receive
the promise in these verses as your own.

ISAIAH 60

No longer will you need the sun to shine by day, nor the moon to give its light by night, for the LORD *your God will be your everlasting light, and your God will be your glory.*

– Isaiah 60:19

At the end of days, I will cause my people to shine brightly. My glory will rest upon you, and you will be radiant and beautiful with my holy light. Once you were forsaken and hated, but my light shining through you makes you majestic. Many people will turn to me because they see how I have made you whole and lovely.

I am your everlasting light. In heaven there is no sun or moon, for my holy brilliance is all you need. My walls are salvation and my gates are praise. In my presence there is no more struggle or sorrow; your days of mourning will end.

This is the end of the story, the final chapter I am writing into your life, and I will make it happen. Let these promises encourage your heart as you wait on me.

Jesus is the Light of the World, in whom is no darkness. He has promised that in heaven we will enjoy the full radiance of his glory as we gaze upon him. As you go about your day, look to him and imagine yourself basking in his light forever.

ISAIAH 61

The Spirit of the Sovereign LORD is upon me, for the LORD has anointed me to bring good news to the poor. He has sent me to comfort the brokenhearted and to proclaim that captives will be released and prisoners will be freed.

– Isaiah 61:1

Do you know why I came to earth?

To bring good news to the poor. To bind up the brokenhearted and proclaim freedom to those held captive by sin. To comfort all who mourn and replace the ashes of sorrow with the oil of gladness. To give my people a cloak of praise instead of a fainting spirit. To make you an oak of righteousness and to glorify myself through you. To repair and build up what has been torn down and devastated.

I came to cause righteousness and praise to spring up from all nations. I have done all of this for you—now go and do it for others! Spread my glory by completing the work I have begun.

This was the passage Jesus quoted about himself at the beginning of his earthly ministry (see Luke 4:18-19). Throughout the Gospels he did these things, proving that he is the Messiah. As you read this chapter, thank God for his ongoing ministry of redemption, and pray that you will see the difficulties you're going through redeemed for his glory and your good.

September
10

ISAIAH 62

Never again will you be called "The Forsaken City" or "The Desolate Land." Your new name will be "The City of God's Delight" and "The Bride of God," for the LORD delights in you and will claim you as his bride.

– Isaiah 62:4

I have made you righteous and given you a new name, written in heaven. You are a crown of beauty to me. No longer are you forsaken or desolate; now you are my delight. I rejoice over you like a groom rejoices over his bride. I have set my love on you, and I will never let you go. You are redeemed. Sought out. Beloved.

Delight in my love as I delight in you. Today, live as someone who has found new love. Think of me often and with great joy. Look forward to the moments you spend with me. Face life with courage because you belong to me and I delight in you.

Those who have trusted in Christ for salvation have been given a new identity: Forgiven. Redeemed. Holy. Chosen. Beloved. Temple of the Holy Spirit. New Creation in Christ. Spend some time in God's presence letting him speak over you the names that represent your new status in him.

ISAIAH 63

I will tell of the LORD's unfailing love. I will praise the LORD
for all he has done. I will rejoice in his great goodness to Israel,
which he has granted according to his mercy and love.

– Isaiah 63:7

No one can match the greatness of my strength or my faithful goodness toward those who love me. I am righteous and mighty to save. Remember how I have shown steadfast love to my people. Don't forget how I rescued Moses and the Israelites at the Red Sea. Ponder how I led them out and gave them rest in the wilderness.

I look down from my holy habitation and am stirred with compassion for you. The same power and mercy that saved Israel from Egypt is available to you, for I am the same righteous Redeemer, mighty to save.

So don't be discouraged. Think on my character and faithfulness, and let that give you reason to hope. I am your loving Savior, strong to save.

This chapter speaks to the dual role of Christ as redeemer of his people and judge of those who reject him. Both aspects of his character are inextricably linked to his holiness. Because God is holy, he must judge sin—but because he is holy he is also able to save those who call to him in faith. Thank God for giving you the gift of salvation.

ISAIAH 64

O LORD, you are our Father. We are the clay, and
you are the potter. We all are formed by your hand.

– Isaiah 64:8

You ask me for big things, and you should—because I can do anything. You ask me to rend the heavens and break into your space and do what you think I should. You remember my mighty acts in the past and beg me to make myself known in the same dramatic ways.

But you forget that I am the potter and you are the clay. I made you who you are, and I am still in the process of molding you into who I want you to be.

So trust me to be good to you. Trust me to do all things well. If my ways seem quiet right now, you can know without a doubt that that's what is best. Wait for me—I am at work even in the silence.

This is an honest and bold prayer for God's help. Read the chapter again slowly and pray these words back to God. What do you long for his help with? Are you submitting to his molding in your life?

ISAIAH 65:17-25

*I will rejoice over Jerusalem and delight in my people. And the
sound of weeping and crying will be heard in it no more.*

– Isaiah 65:19

I am making a new heaven and a new earth, and they will be places of eternal rejoicing. When I return, you will not even remember the pain you've experienced in this life, and the joy you've had so far will pale in comparison to the radiant joy you will have then.

There will be no more distress, no more weeping, no more death, no more hurt or destruction. You will live in my house and enjoy good, satisfying work and glorious worship at my throne. Even the natural order will be completely new, with the wolf and the lamb grazing together without fear.

Rejoice in this certain hope that awaits you. Even today, live in the reality that better things are in store for you than you can even imagine.

What a beautiful picture Isaiah gives of heaven. Make a list of all God's promises that are mentioned here. Let these words give you deep joy today, and hope that triumphs over every heartache.

September 14

ISAIAH 66:1-2, 12-14

*My hands have made both heaven and earth; they and everything
in them are mine. I, the LORD, have spoken! I will bless those
who have humble and contrite hearts, who tremble at my word.*

– Isaiah 66:2

Heaven is my throne, and the earth is my footstool. I have made everything that is, and I rule over all things.

Yet I dwell with those who are humble and contrite in spirit, with those who read my Word and tremble over their sin. I, the King of heaven and Creator of all, come to you when you humble yourself before me. I make your heart my temple and live in you by my Spirit.

When you delight yourself in me, I make peace flow out of you like a river. I comfort you as a mother comforts her child. You flourish and bear fruit, for my blessing rests on my servants.

The promises of these verses hinge on our humility before God (verse 2). Have you humbled yourself before him? Do you have a repentant heart, one that trembles at his Word? If not, perhaps a good place to start is by meditating on verse 1 and keeping a picture of God's greatness at the forefront of your mind.

September 15

JEREMIAH 1:5-10

I knew you before I formed you in your mother's womb. Before you were born I set you apart and appointed you as my prophet to the nations.

– Jeremiah 1:5

Before I formed you in your mother's womb, I knew you. I had already set you apart for the work I have for you. Nothing happens to you outside my appointed plan.

So don't say this job is too big for you—I made you for it. Don't say that you can't accomplish the task I have given you—it was created for you before you even existed. Don't look at the size of the task, look at the size of your God.

I will help you to accomplish my will. I will put my words in your mouth and lift you up to the right position. I am the one who destroys and the one who builds up. Trust me that I will work my will in and through you, and do not fear.

God made us with great care and love, and he gave us just the right set of characteristics and gifts to accomplish what he wants us to do. He also prepared in advance the tasks he will give us (see Ephesians 2:10). Do you trust him enough to walk forward into whatever he's calling you to do? Or are you shrinking back in fear because you're relying on your own strength?

JEREMIAH 4:1-4

*Plow up the hard ground of your hearts! . . . Surrender your
pride and power. Change your hearts before the LORD.*

– J e r e m i a h   4 : 3 - 4

Return to me, dear one. Remove from your life the things you have
worshiped instead of me. Throw them away! Don't make allowance
for your evil—banish it from your life.

Break up the fallow ground in your heart. Plant the seeds of my Word
there, and water it so it flourishes and bears fruit in your life. Surrender
your pride and relinquish your power, submitting your desires to me.
Devote yourself to me alone.

When you give yourself wholly to me, I will abide with you. We will
have sweet fellowship, with no barriers between us, and you will be at
peace.

These verses are a tender invitation into a deeper walk with the
Lord. Throw away your idols and soften your heart toward him.
Talk to him about the things that are holding you back from
radical transformation, and then take action to uproot those
things from your life.

JEREMIAH 10:1-16

LORD, there is no one like you! For you are great, and your name is full of power. Who would not fear you, O King of nations? . . . Among all the wise people of the earth and in all the kingdoms of the world, there is no one like you.

– Jeremiah 10:6-7

Don't follow the ways of the world around you. Don't worship their idols or fear what they fear.

There is no one like me, mighty in power and able to do great things. I am the only true God, the living and everlasting King. I made the earth by my power, and I established the world by my wisdom. I stretched out the heavens. At the sound of my voice, the sea rises in tumult or falls silent and still. The whole earth is filled with the trailing edges of my glory, and the air is perfumed with the presence of my holiness.

I am big and you are small. Therefore, trust me—not yourself. Live by my wisdom, not your own. Take my gentle correction and follow my commandments so it will go well with you.

Peer pressure doesn't end when we become adults. We want to fit in, and we covet all the good things other people seem to have. Purpose today to turn your back on the world's values and cling to Christ, to reject the idols other people worship and instead serve the true God.

September 18

JEREMIAH 15:19-20

*If you return to me, I will restore you so you can
continue to serve me. If you speak good words
rather than worthless ones, you will be my spokesman.*

– Jeremiah 15:19

Turn back to me, beloved. See what I will do if you come to me: I will restore you to sweet relationship with me. I will cause you to stand before me, forgiven and declared righteous.

I will give you my message to speak to others. You will have a noble purpose, a job to do that matters. I will make you like a strong wall, and no one will be able to prevail against you, for I will be with you. I will save you and deliver you, for I am the Lord. All these things I will do for you if you will only turn back to me in humility, bowing your heart before me in worship and love.

This verse highlights the responsibility we bear in our spiritual productivity. We must return in order for God to restore us, and we must speak good words rather than worthless ones. But God does the bulk of the work: He restores us to himself, and he makes us his ambassadors. Won't you do your little part so God can do big things through you?

JEREMIAH 17:5-14

*O Lord, if you heal me, I will be truly healed; if you save
me, I will be truly saved. My praises are for you alone!*

– Jeremiah 17:14

It is useless to trust in the strength of people—mere mortals—to save you. They can't even save themselves, so how can they save you? Only I can save you. So don't turn your heart away from me. Don't forsake the fountain of living water. If you do, you will be like a dry shrub in the desert. Your soul will shrivel and die. You will feel like you're in a parched wilderness or an uninhabited salt land.

If you want happiness and blessing, trust in me. Draw your life from me. Then you will be like a tree planted by water. Your roots will have plenty of fresh water to drink, and your soul will thrive even on hot days. You will not have reason to be anxious, because you will continue to bear fruit even in difficult circumstances. I will heal you and save you.

The people of Judah worshiped idols and placed their trust in mortals. They were about to be taken captive at the Lord's command. But there was still hope—if they turned from their idols and placed their trust in the Lord, they would be like lush green trees. Do you long for deeper life and more of God? Reject your idols and place your hope in the Lord, and he will heal and restore you from the inside out.

JEREMIAH 23

"For the time is coming," says the LORD, "when I will raise up a righteous descendant from King David's line. He will be a King who rules with wisdom. He will do what is just and right throughout the land."

– Jeremiah 23:5

My true shepherds are the ones who speak my Word. They care for my people, and as a result of their good teaching, my people know me and have no reason to fear.

But there are many false teachers. Their course is evil, and they do despicable things. They are adulterers and drunks who live to satisfy their own appetites. They give you vain hope and speak visions from their own minds, not from me. One day they will receive justice for the way they have led my people astray.

I am a God who is close. No one can hide in secret places where I do not see, for I fill heaven and earth. I see the prophets who prophesy lies, and I will cast them away to everlasting shame. But I also see those whose hearts are steadfastly devoted to me, and those people I will protect and sustain forever.

You can probably think of a few so-called Christian preachers and church leaders who fit Jeremiah's description of false prophets. Fortunately, even when human leaders disappoint or even devastate us, God never lets us down. He is the Good Shepherd, and we can trust him completely.

September
21

JEREMIAH 24:4-7

I will give them hearts that recognize me as the LORD. They will be my people, and I will be their God, for they will return to me wholeheartedly.

– Jeremiah 24:7

The people who truly know me are blessed. I set my eyes on them for good, and I build them up in love. They are planted and established in the land, and I give them a heart to know me. They are my people, and I am their God, for their whole hearts are devoted to me.

Abide in me, the true vine, so you can bear good fruit. Stay close to me and you will live in my blessing and protection. The secret to a rich, full life is to simply abide—to seek more of me. Breathe in grace, breathe out praise.

This prophecy was made concerning the Jews who had been exiled to Babylon. They were living as captives in enemy territory, yet they were better off than those who were left in Jerusalem because they trusted the Lord, and he would take care of them and cause them to bear fruit. No matter where you are, God can make you fruitful for the gospel.

JEREMIAH 29:1-14

*Work for the peace and prosperity of the city where I sent you into exile.
Pray to the LORD for it, for its welfare will determine your welfare.*

– Jeremiah 29:7

You have found yourself in a place you didn't expect, a place you would not have chosen. Some days it feels like exile.

This is where I have planted you for this time. Build your house and live well here. Plant a garden, expecting to be here for the harvest. Establish and grow your family. The key to living well in a season of exile is to seek the welfare of the place where I have planted you, so pray for the people here. Invest in relationships with them and tell them about me.

I know the plans I have for you in this place, and they are plans for your good, not for evil. With me, you have a future and a hope. Seek me and ask me what I have for you. I will show you how to make this place your home rather than a place of exile. And best of all, I myself will be your true home, your eternal home, so that no matter where you are on earth, you can find security and belonging in me.

These words written to the Jewish exiles can apply to us as well, because we are strangers on this earth, citizens of heaven (see Hebrews 13:14). We should diligently work for the good of the place where God has planted us, even though this world is not our true home.

JEREMIAH 30:8-22

"In that day," says the LORD of Heaven's Armies, "I will break the yoke from their necks and snap their chains. Foreigners will no longer be their masters. For my people will serve the LORD their God and their king descended from David—the king I will raise up for them."

– Jeremiah 30:8-9

I have broken the bonds of your slavery to sin. Death no longer sits on your neck like a heavy yoke. I have given you quiet and ease in your salvation, for it is all a gift of grace rather than a result of your own good works.

I am with you to save you. I will bring you from a place of hurt and shame to full health. I will heal your wounds. I have disciplined you in love, and now I will restore you. Soon you will raise your voice in songs of thanksgiving at all I have done for you.

This is what it means that you are mine, and I am your God. I give you freedom and peace and healing and joy—things that are true and deep in your soul even if the world around you is falling apart. Hold on to these promises and live them with joy.

Think of the Israelites' freedom from captivity as a metaphor for your freedom from sin, bought by Christ's substitutionary sacrifice. How does thinking of it this way help you appreciate more deeply the amazing gift of salvation?

JEREMIAH 31:1-14

I have loved you, my people, with an everlasting love.
With unfailing love I have drawn you to myself.

— Jeremiah 31:3

You can find grace even in the wilderness if you seek me. When you seek my rest, I will draw near to you.

For I love you with a never-ending, always-for-you love. I am faithful to you. I am the one who helps you build and plant and provide for yourself and your loved ones.

When you come to me with weeping, I will comfort you and give you a glad heart. I will lead you to the waters of life and make a straight path for your feet so you do not stumble. Your mourning shall be turned to joy because you are ransomed and redeemed, bought with my blood and forever my beloved. Dance with joy and delight in my good gifts. Let your soul feast on my abundant goodness.

Jesus is the one who brings final and complete fulfillment to these promises. Choose one of the images of restoration from this chapter to meditate on throughout the day, and thank God for the hope we have in heaven.

September
25

JEREMIAH 31:17-34

You disciplined me severely, like a calf that needs training for the yoke.
Turn me again to you and restore me, for you alone are the LORD my God.

– Jeremiah 31:18

There is hope for your future. You have been disciplined, and now is the time for restoration. You wandered away from me, but I drew you back with my love. Come to me and be healed.

Now that you are back on the right path, set up markers in your life that will point you back to me when you are tempted to stray from my love. Choose me, over and over again, moment by moment—choose me.

You can be faithful to me because I have changed you from the inside out. The Holy Spirit—I myself—live in you and empower you. You can know me and serve me because I am with you, helping you each step of the way. Trust in me and my power; you don't have to do this in your own strength.

Think of a time God disciplined you. What form did that discipline take? What good came out of it? Thank God for being a loving heavenly Father who does not leave us in our sin but calls us back to the path of life.

September

26

JEREMIAH 33:1-16

This is what the LORD says—the LORD who made the earth, who formed and established it, whose name is the LORD: Ask me and I will tell you remarkable secrets you do not know about things to come.

– Jeremiah 33:2-3

Call to me and I will answer you. I will reveal to you great things, showing you my ways and my will for you. What a great future is in store for you! When you see it, you will tremble because of how good it is.

One day I will return to bring justice and righteousness to the earth. My people will dwell securely in the city called "the Lord Is Our Righteousness." The streets will be filled with rejoicing as the people praise me for my steadfast love. There will be rest and peace under the rule of Jesus, the forever King. That is your true home, where your true citizenship is.

Life on earth is temporary, and your sojourn here is brief. So focus on and work for that great final day when I will return and restore all things.

God is working out his long-range plan by which as many people as possible will come to a saving knowledge of him. Ask him today to give you a glimpse of what he's doing in the world. Then ask if there is some way you can join in his great rescue plan.

LAMENTATIONS 3

*Yet I still dare to hope when I remember this: The faithful love
of the LORD never ends! His mercies never cease. Great is his
faithfulness; his mercies begin afresh each morning. I say to myself,
"The LORD is my inheritance; therefore, I will hope in him!"*

– Lamentations 3:21-24

You have borne great affliction. Sorrow has filled your days, and weeping has filled your nights. You were afflicted and wandering in darkness. I have seen it all, and I have wept with you in your deep grief.

Now is the time to rise up. Say these truths to your burdened soul: "The steadfast love of the Lord never ceases. His mercies never end. Each morning they spring up new, for God is faithful."

I am your portion and your hope, and I am enough. When you remind yourself of the abundance of my steadfast love, you will have an anchor of hope for your soul. Wait quietly for me and hope in me, for your salvation is sure.

It is daring to hold on to hope in the face of darkness, isn't it? But if we keep reminding ourselves of the truth that God is faithful and good—all the time—we can anchor our souls in deep, abiding hope.

September
28

EZEKIEL 11:16-20; 36:22-27; 37:23-28

I will take away their stony, stubborn heart and give them a tender,
responsive heart, so they will obey my decrees and regulations.
Then they will truly be my people, and I will be their God.

– E z e k i e l   1 1 : 1 9 - 2 0

I am your sanctuary, your safe place. I gather you near, replacing your angry, stubborn heart of stone with a heart of flesh that responds to me. I do the work of renewing you and causing your soul to grow in me. All you have to do is come to me.

I do this not because you deserve it—for you never could. I sanctify you for my sake, to glorify my name. This is how I keep my promise to make a people for myself. I gather you in, sprinkle you clean, and give you a new heart. I give you my Spirit to help you obey me and to seal you as my own dear child.

This is my everlasting covenant of peace: I will live in your heart, and you will be my dwelling place. My home is with you.

The exiles probably thought what they needed most was political freedom. But what they really needed is the same thing we really need—a new heart and peace with God. Spiritual freedom is of far more value than physical or political freedom. Ask God to soften your heart toward him today.

EZEKIEL 34:11-31

You are my flock, the sheep of my pasture. You are my people,
and I am your God. I, the Sovereign LORD, have spoken!

– Ezekiel 34:31

I search high and low for my sheep, seeking them out from their hiding places. I follow you everywhere you try to run so I can tenderly bring you back home, out of danger. I rescue you from your places of wandering and return you to safety.

I feed you in good pasture. You can lie down and rest, for I myself give you a safe place to lie down. I bind up your wounds when you are hurt and strengthen you when you are weak. I give you cool, clear water to refresh your soul.

This is what I do for my sheep, because I am the Good Shepherd. I have made a covenant of peace with you so you can dwell securely in the place of my blessing. Whatever you need today, you can trust that I will give it to you because I am your Good Shepherd.

Meditate on all the ways God is a good shepherd to you. How has he sought you? Fed you? Strengthened you? Refreshed you? Given you a secure place to live? Blessed you? Thank him today.

JOEL 2:12-14, 28-32

Don't tear your clothing in your grief, but tear your hearts instead. Return to the LORD your God, for he is merciful and compassionate, slow to get angry and filled with unfailing love. He is eager to relent and not punish.

– J o e l 2 : 1 3

You wonder if this time you've gone too far. Are you outside of my grace? Was this one time too many for me to forgive the same sin?

It is never too late. Even now, return to me. Rend your heart. Mourn over your sin. Test me, and see if I am not gracious and merciful, abounding in steadfast love. I will open my hand and shower blessings on you—salvation, reconciliation, and peace.

Come before me in humility, and I will pour out my Spirit on you, for everyone who calls on my name will be saved. You will see wonders as never before, if only you will repent.

People who don't really know God accuse him of being angry and condemning. But the truth is, when we take the single step of repenting of our sin, he eagerly welcomes us back. He loves to forgive and is filled with unfailing love. Have you met the true God described in these verses and allowed him to pour out his Spirit on you?

October

MICAH 6:7-8; 7:7, 18-20

*The LORD has told you what is good, and this is what he requires of you:
to do what is right, to love mercy, and to walk humbly with your God.*

– Micah 6:8

D o you think I want all your acts of service, all your gifts of money? What I really want is your obedience. I want a heart that is humble before me and devoted to doing my will. If your heart is mine, then your service and giving is an act of worship, and I will receive it as such. But if your heart is not mine, then your good deeds are like filthy rags. It is not the outward acts that please me, but the inward bent of your heart.

I am the God who pardons your iniquity and forgives you. I do not keep anger, because I delight in you with steadfast love. The moment you repent, I look on you with compassion and cast your sins into the depths of the sea. I am your faithful God, abounding in steadfast love toward you.

This is one of those verses that makes the Christian life sound pretty simple. But some days it is hard to do what is right and walk humbly with the Lord. The good news is, God is faithful and abounds in steadfast love toward you. When you fail, he picks you up again, every time.

October
2

HABAKKUK

Even though the fig trees have no blossoms, and there are no grapes on the
vines; even though the olive crop fails, and the fields lie empty and barren . . .
yet I will rejoice in the LORD! I will be joyful in the God of my salvation!

– Habakkuk 3:17-18

If you could only see what I see, if you could pull back the veil of the future, you would be astounded. You wouldn't even believe it if I told you what is in store for you. I am from everlasting, the holy judge, and I am setting everything right in its time. My mercy is coming.

So even though it seems as if all hope is lost, even though you can't see that I am doing anything, even though there is no bud on the tree, trust me. Live by faith, not by sight.

One day the earth will be filled with the knowledge of my glory as waters cover the sea. Everyone will bow down and worship me, and the nations will tremble before me. Rejoice and take courage in this certain hope as you trust in me to keep my promises.

Habakkuk is a dialogue between the prophet, who doubts God's goodness when so much is going wrong, and God, who assures Habakkuk that he is working out his perfect will. If you don't have time to read the whole book, read chapter 3 and be encouraged that our merciful God is doing amazing things and we can trust him, even when we are filled with doubt.

October

3

ZEPHANIAH 3

For the LORD your God is living among you. He is a mighty savior. He will take delight in you with gladness. With his love, he will calm all your fears. He will rejoice over you with joyful songs.

– Zephaniah 3:17

I am the righteous and mighty one in your midst, active in your world. Every moment, without fail, I do what is right. I am bringing justice to the earth in my time; one day soon I will return and set everything right. This is the promise you can cling to when the days are dark.

But even now, while you are still in this troubled world, you can have hope. I am with you. Come to me and let me quiet your anxious heart with my love. Let me calm you as I sing over you with joyful songs. I will gather you close and restore your joy.

If you're worried about something today or just feel far from God, spend time in his presence and imagine him singing joyful songs over you. He loves you, and you bring great delight to his heart.

October

4

ZECHARIAH 2:13-3:9; 9:9, 16-17

On that day the LORD their God will rescue his people, just as a shepherd rescues his sheep. They will sparkle in his land like jewels in a crown.

– Zechariah 9:16

Be silent before me, for I am in my holy dwelling, poised to act. My eternal purpose is to save the people I have made, and that is what I am doing even now. I am your righteous and humble King, riding to you in victory.

I removed your filthy garments and washed away your sin. I gave you clean clothes to wear, robes of righteousness. Rejoice, for my salvation has come to you. All the accusations Satan has made against you are refuted, for I have forgiven your sin.

Now you have a new identity: Saved. Pure. Holy. Jewel shining in the land. I have placed on you my goodness and beauty. This is who you are, your identity for all eternity, so live like the holy child you are.

The New Testament talks about putting off our old nature and putting on our new nature (see Ephesians 4:22-24). In one sense God already did this for us at the moment of salvation, but in another sense we have to take daily action to put to death the deeds of darkness and put on the clothing of righteousness. Live like the holy jewel you are in Christ.

MALACHI 3:6, 16-4:3

*But for you who fear my name, the Sun of Righteousness
will rise with healing in his wings. And you will go free,
leaping with joy like calves let out to pasture.*

– Malachi 4:2

I am the Lord, and I do not change. That is why you are not consumed, for I am a gracious God, abounding in steadfast love and faithfulness. I have written your name in the Book of Life. You are my treasured possession, my own dear child. Your future is secure because I have saved you.

Because you love and honor me, I rise up to you with healing in my wings. You are protected and rescued, safe in the Day of Judgment. I have freed you from sin and death. I have bound your wounds and helped you to stand, full and complete and forgiven. Once you were stooped and crippled by sin, but now you can leap like a calf released from its stall.

These promises are for those who fear the Lord and meditate on his name (3:16). Looking over your life in the past week, do you fear the Lord and meditate on, or think honorably about, his name? How can you grow in these areas?

October
6

LUKE 1:46-55

The Mighty One is holy, and he has done great things for me.

– Luke 1:49

Let your soul magnify me. Let your spirit rejoice, for I have seen your need and raised you up. I have done great things for you, and my name is holy.

I show mercy to those who call on me in humility. I shower blessings on the generations of those who serve me. With my strong arm I bring down the proud and raise up the lowly.

When you hunger for me, I fill you with good things. Those who think they have no need for me go away empty, but all who truly seek me are filled to overflowing with my love and grace. Come, eat, and drink your fill from the source of life.

What great things has God done for you? Has he done for you some of the things Mary sings about in this song? Praise him for all his mighty and holy acts.

October

7

LUKE 1:68-79

Because of God's tender mercy, the morning light from heaven is about to break upon us, to give light to those who sit in darkness and in the shadow of death, and to guide us to the path of peace.

– Luke 1:78-79

I have visited and redeemed my people. I came to you to save you from sin and death, just as I promised I would. Yes, I have kept every promise.

I remembered my covenant and showed you mercy. I made it so you can serve me without fear, for you have been declared righteous and holy through me.

I have given you knowledge of my salvation, the ability to understand my offer of forgiveness. The sunrise has visited you from on high because of my tender mercy. Now you walk in the way of peace, reconciled to your Creator and living under my loving care for all eternity.

The verses above summarize what Jesus did by coming to earth. Think about Jesus' life, death, and resurrection in light of this description. Do any new insights come from thinking of it in these terms?

JOHN 3:1-21

This is how God loved the world: He gave his one and only
Son, so that everyone who believes in him will not perish
but have eternal life. God sent his Son into the world not
to judge the world, but to save the world through him.

– John 3:16-17

From the moment your life began, you were under the curse of sin and death. You could do nothing to save yourself, and you could not keep yourself from doing wrong.

That is why you must be born again to eternal life, born of water and the Spirit. I gave my only Son to bring life to your doomed soul. Jesus came not to judge, but to save. It is the greatest offer that could be made—exchange your sin for holiness, dark for light, death for life.

Yet the world rejected him, preferring to stumble in the darkness rather than come into the light. Don't make the same mistake. You can be raised to new life simply by believing in me. Choose me, choose life and light. Only believe, and you will be saved.

Sometimes salvation becomes so familiar to us that we take it for granted. Today, spend some time meditating on the gift of salvation as Jesus described it to Nicodemus. Try to receive it as if for the first time and ask the Holy Spirit to breathe fresh life into your love for Jesus.

October

9

JOHN 4:1-30

Anyone who drinks this water will soon become thirsty again.
But those who drink the water I give will never be thirsty again.
It becomes a fresh, bubbling spring within them, giving them eternal life.

– John 4:13-14

Here is a gift you can have anytime you wish: living water—soul nourishment. Because you have trusted in me, the Holy Spirit lives within you, bubbling up with life and offering refreshment for you and everyone you meet.

When you drink of me, taking nourishment from my Word, your every spiritual need will be met. You don't need to suffer from soul thirst that dries you up inside. You have within you a spring of Spirit life welling up to eternal life. The kind of life he offers is deep satisfaction and joy, wholeness and truth.

Won't you come and drink of me? Come to the fountain of living water. Drink and be satisfied, today and forever.

What are you thirsty for today? What are you longing for? Turn those desires and longings back to Jesus, the only one who truly satisfies. Ask him to show you how your desires can be met in him.

MATTHEW 18:21-35

"Lord, how often should I forgive someone who sins against me? Seven times?" "No, not seven times," Jesus replied, "but seventy times seven!"

– Matthew 18:21-22

Do you truly understand what I have done for you? Your sin was much greater than you can ever comprehend. Your debt to me was immense. All the rebellion, selfishness, idol worship . . . and I forgave it all.

Those who have contemplated the extent of their sin can better understand my love for them. So today, think for a while about your sin. Repent. Confess before me all the ways you have rejected and forgotten me. Call your selfishness what it is—sin against me.

Then receive my full forgiveness. Rejoice that you have been made holy. Give thanks that I washed you white as snow. And let my grace move you to extend to others the same forgiveness I have given you.

Forgive as you have been forgiven.

It's easy to forget how great our debt of sin is. Read through this passage again, and put yourself into the story. How are you like the servant? Then spend time in confession and receive God's forgiveness.

MARK 2:1-12; LUKE 5:17-26

Seeing their faith, Jesus said to the paralyzed man,
"My child, your sins are forgiven."

– M a r k   2 : 5

I see how your heart breaks for your friends who don't know me. I see your longing for them to be forgiven and made whole.

Keep bringing them before me in prayer. Be like the friends of the paralytic and bring to me those who can't bring themselves. It is your faith that can make the difference in their lives, so don't give up. Don't stop asking me to help them.

Even today I am at work, calling those who are far from me to saving faith. One day you will say, "I have seen extraordinary things. People I thought would never come to Jesus have been saved." Keep praying, keep faithfully telling others about my love, and see what I will do. I am the Savior who redeems helpless, hopeless sinners.

We can learn many important lessons from this story, but one is that our faith can benefit our friends. Think of the friend you are most concerned for, and spend time in prayer, bringing them before the Lord and asking him to meet their deepest needs. Enlist the help of mutual friends and keep praying in the coming weeks and months.

October

12

LUKE 5:27-32; MARK 2:12-17

Healthy people don't need a doctor—sick people do. I have come to call not those who think they are righteous, but those who know they are sinners and need to repent.

– Luke 5:31-32

I didn't come to save those who think they can save themselves. I came for the lost, for sinners, for those who are in desperate need. I came for you. I came for your friends. And I came for the people you think are unworthy of my love.

Do you know you are sick? Do you know that apart from me you are without hope? Contemplate who you were before I saved you, who you would be without my grace, and then let it move you to have compassion for others. Let it compel you to reach out to "the least of these." Let it encourage you to humility as you realize you are no more worthy of my love than the worst murderer.

Think of someone you believe is despicable. Now pray for them. Ask God to save them in the same way he saved Levi, and then see if God is asking you to befriend them to share the love of Jesus with them.

MATTHEW 9:14-17; LUKE 5:33-39

*Who would patch old clothing with new cloth? For the
new patch would shrink and rip away from the old
cloth, leaving an even bigger tear than before.*

– Matthew 9:16

When I came to you, I brought with me a new covenant. It was a covenant of peace rather than law. A covenant in my blood rather than the blood of sacrifices. A covenant of repentance rather than good works.

The old covenant pointed out your sin and your need for a savior. Now, the Savior has come. You can be free from the laws and regulations because I met the law's demands on your behalf.

My grace can't be measured or contained. Don't try to put the covenant of life back into the same container that held the covenant of law and death—it won't fit. Rejoice that I came, and live in your new freedom!

The old covenant was the law, and the new covenant is grace. Jesus came and fulfilled the old covenant's requirements on our behalf so we can live free from the law's restraints. We are already saved, apart from the law. Now we can obey from a heart of love, rather than from obligation.

October
14

JOHN 5:1-15

When Jesus saw him and knew he had been ill for a long time, he asked him, "Would you like to get well?"

– J o h n 5 : 6

D o you want to be healed? It seems like a silly question—of course you do! But healing requires that you leave the old, comfortable ways. You have to leave what you know and step into unfamiliar territory. You must accept a new identity, and that can be scary.

The healing I offer to you is soul healing, the forgiveness of sin, and restoration of your relationship with me. It is spiritual blessing poured out in your heart and everlasting joy. That's what you need more than physical healing.

If you want to be made well, reach out to me. The healing I give is full and complete, and it lasts for all eternity. Don't be afraid of starting a new life with me. The paths I will take you on are ways of peace, and I will be with you every step of the way. Come and walk in newness of life!

Contemplate Jesus' question, "Would you like to get well?" (verse 6). Why do you think he asked that? Now think about the man's evasive response. He was pointing out the barriers to healing, and not really answering the question. Now answer the question for yourself—think of all the places where you need healing, and ask yourself if you really want to get well. Then ask God to heal you.

October

15

MATTHEW 5:1-12

God blesses those who are poor and realize their need for him.

– Matthew 5:3

You think of blessing as prosperity, but true blessing is spiritual, not material. And it comes in unexpected ways:

Blessed are the poor in spirit, those who are desperate and humble before me, for they will have eternal life. Blessed are those who sorrow, for I comfort them and give them peace. Blessed are those who gently serve others, for they will receive back blessing from me. Blessed are those who hunger and thirst for righteousness, for I will satisfy their longing for spiritual growth.

Blessed are those who show mercy when they are mistreated, for they will receive mercy. Blessed are those who come to me to be purified, for they will see me. Blessed are the peacemakers, for they will increasingly reflect my character. Blessed are those who are persecuted because they associate themselves with me, for they have an eternal inheritance that far outshines anything this world can offer. The way down is the way further in; come and be blessed.

According to these verses, the blessed life comes at a cost. Are you ready for this kind of blessing?

October
16

MATTHEW 5:13-16;
MARK 4:21-25; LUKE 8:16-18

Let your good deeds shine out for all to see,
so that everyone will praise your heavenly Father.

– Matthew 5:16

Think of all I have done for you—I took you while you were still dead and gave you life. I saved you while you were still my enemy, and I offer that same salvation to anyone who comes to me in faith. This good news is not meant to be kept to yourself. Share it! Be like salt, making others thirsty for me.

I am the Light of the World, and as you spend time with me and learn more about me, you reflect my light and shine it into the world. No one lights a lamp and then covers it up. Instead, they put it in a prominent place so it can fulfill its purpose to illuminate the entire room. Don't hide what I have done for you or cover the light I have placed within you. Love others enough to shine my light for all to see.

Let your good works shine out so that others will glorify me. Don't hide in embarrassment or fear, but rather proclaim the Good News that I love the world and offer salvation to anyone who turns to me.

In what ways are you letting your light shine so that others will praise God? In what ways are you hiding your light under a bushel? Ask God to shine his light through you this week.

MATTHEW 5:17-48

You are to be perfect, even as your Father in heaven is perfect.

– Matthew 5:48

I came to fulfill the law, and I accomplished everything it required. I obeyed all the Father asked so I could be a perfect sacrifice, paying the penalty you owed for your sin. I've paid that price, but that doesn't mean you have license to do anything you want.

The law said do not murder, but I tell you that being angry with someone is against the law of love. You think if you don't commit adultery you are doing well, but I say that if you have lustful intent in your heart you have already broken my law. You think it's enough to love your neighbor, but I say you must love your enemy and pray for the person who mistreats you.

Who then can be saved? How can anyone keep my commandments? Apart from me, no one can. But I offer you my righteousness, my perfection. I kept the law and now impute to you my holiness, and I give you the Holy Spirit to empower you to obey me. Receive these gifts with thanksgiving, and then let them move you from a heart of love to keep my commandments.

The verse above sounds intimidating until we remember that we are made perfect through the work of Jesus at the cross. All the same, these verses command us to live with a challenging— even impossible—depth of love and obedience. Thank God for fulfilling the law on your behalf, and then purpose to obey him deeply and fully.

LUKE 15

There is joy in the presence of God's angels when even one sinner repents.

– Luke 15:10

Do you know what causes us to throw a party in heaven? The repentance of a sinner. My greatest joy is saving helpless people. That is why I run after the lost sheep rather than stay with the ninety-nine who are already in the flock.

The prodigal who has run far away from me, when he comes to his senses and returns to me, will find that I have flung my arms open wide to welcome him back. I have been waiting for that one, and I celebrate his return with great joy.

Do you resent this joy of mine? Do you think I should not lavish such celebration on people you believe are unworthy? Leave your anger behind. All that I have is yours, and this celebration is for you as well. Come and rejoice over the new life that has come to those who were dead, over the finding of what was lost and the redemption of an eternal soul. Don't hold back and stand in judgment, for the only one missing out is you. Celebrate with me the birth of new life for the most impossible sinner.

These three parables demonstrate God's heart for sinners. Do you share his concern for the lost? Pray that you will have his heart for lost souls, and then look for opportunities today to share his love with someone who doesn't yet know him.

MATTHEW 6:1-4

Give your gifts in private, and your Father,
who sees everything, will reward you.

– M a t t h e w 6 : 4

I know your heart. You can't hide your motives from me, and you probably can't hide them from as many people as you think you can. Most people can detect hypocrisy, and it profanes my holy name.

Don't do good things to be seen by people. Don't give in order to make people admire you. Don't call attention to your generosity or publish your righteous deeds so that others will tell you what a good person you are. If you do, that is all the reward you'll receive.

Instead, do your good deeds in secret. Give anonymously. Work behind the scenes rather than seeking the spotlight. Let your reward be in heaven, not on earth. Live to please me, not the people around you. I am the only audience who matters.

Is it harder for you to give when no one will ever know about your generosity? Think of someone to whom you can give an anonymous gift, and then do it today.

October

20

MATTHEW 6:25-34; LUKE 12:22-34

Don't worry about tomorrow, for tomorrow will bring
its own worries. Today's trouble is enough for today.

– Matthew 6:34

It's easy to find things to be anxious about. You worry about whether you'll have enough money in the bank or whether your job is secure. You worry about the next deadline or the next medical test. You worry about those you love.

But the truth is, you don't need to worry. I take care of everything I have made. Even the lilies of the field are clothed in beauty, and the birds have plenty to eat, even though they don't store anything up for tomorrow. You are of so much more value than these things, and I know what you need even before you do.

Seek first my Kingdom, and let me take care of all the other details of your life. Trust me to take care of tomorrow. Set aside your anxiety, for it is my pleasure to care for your every need. I'll even care for many of your desires—those seemingly unimportant things you long for—because I love to give good gifts to my children.

The Bible tells us more than one hundred times not to fear. Add in verses about being at peace or fearing God rather than men, and you get close to 365, one per day. Take that admonition to heart and turn your worries over to God. Meditate on these passages and try to live in the moment, trusting God to take care of the future.

MATTHEW 11:28-30

My yoke is easy to bear, and the burden I give you is light.

– Matthew 11:30

Are you weighed down with life's stresses? Feeling tired and run-down and ready to give up? Exhausted from trying to get it all right? Continually overwhelmed by work and worry?

Come to me, and I will give you deep soul rest. I don't ask you to earn salvation; I give it freely. You can let go of your restless striving and simply rest in me. Stop trying so hard and trust in my finished work at the cross and my promise to complete what I have begun in you. I don't require of you things you can't do, for everything I call you to, I equip you for. Cease all your doing for me and simply be with me—that's what I really want from you.

My yoke is discipleship, imitating my example and learning from me in close relationship. All I ask is that you follow me. Spend time with me, breathing in my presence and basking in my glory. I am gentle with you, and I call you to rest and peace.

If you're feeling overwhelmed, that's a sign that you are taking on your own yoke rather than that of Christ. Meditate on these words as you think of both the responsibility you feel for your spiritual life and the daily tasks you're taking on. In what areas do you need to give up your own yoke and take on Christ's light, restful burden?

MATTHEW 13:1-23

The seed that fell on good soil represents those who truly hear
and understand God's word and produce a harvest of thirty,
sixty, or even a hundred times as much as had been planted!

– Matthew 13:23

Plow the field of your heart, uprooting sin so you are prepared to receive my Word. Don't let Satan snatch my words away before they can sprout and grow. Don't allow your heart to get hardened and stony, so that truth can't grow deep roots there. You don't want shallow faith that will wither away in the heat of trials. Finally, don't let your heart be filled with the cares of this world so that your faith is choked out.

When my Word enters your heart, let it find fertile soul. Feed yourself with Scripture. Grow deep roots through time spent with me. Let truth flourish and bear fruit in your life. Then you will produce a crop, even a hundred times what was planted.

We can think of this parable in terms of evangelism, which is the main context of the passage, and also in terms of the soil in our own hearts. Consider each type of soil and contemplate ways in which your heart may be hard or infertile. Pray for your heart and for the hearts of the people in your sphere of influence to be receptive to God's Word.

October

23

MATTHEW 8:23-27; MARK 4:35-41

When Jesus woke up, he rebuked the wind and said to the waves,
"Silence! Be still!" Suddenly the wind stopped, and there was a great calm.

– Mark 4:39

I see the storm that's coming. I'm not asleep on the job, not unaware of the imminent danger you see. I am not taken by surprise by these waves and swells that seem to you to come without warning.

But I also see the bigger picture. I am the one who commands the wind and the seas. I am in control of every circumstance of your life—even this. At the right moment, I will say to these raging seas, "Peace! Be still!" and the storm will cease. It has no choice, for I am the Lord of All.

Don't wait until the storm is over to release your fear to me. Even now, as the storm clouds gather overhead, show me your faith. Refuse to give in to fear, and choose faith and hope instead. Trust that I am the Lord who is in control and that I will keep you safe and do good to you.

Imagine yourself on the boat with Jesus. Imagine the storms around you, and specifically name the things that frighten you right now. Let Jesus calm those storms and build your faith by his presence and his gentle word.

MARK 7:1–23

You skillfully sidestep God's law in order to hold on to your own tradition.
— Mark 7:10

People may tell you that you have to follow certain regulations and rules to worship me. They want to place careful boundaries around your relationship with me because they are afraid of doing the wrong thing, as if your deeds of righteousness are what secures your salvation. Or they try to exercise power over you by making new rules, adding to what I have commanded and placing themselves in authority over me.

What I want is your heart, not your outward acts of piety. It is your inner life that determines whether you are pure or defiled. The things you say and do are an overflow of what is truly in your heart.

Seek purity from the inside out. Set your heart on me, and good things will flow out of you. Everything you do in my name and for my glory will be an act of worship. Don't worry so much about the externals; concern yourself with keeping your heart in tune with mine.

The Pharisees thought they had this religion thing all figured out—obey their man-made laws and they would please God. But Jesus told them that they weren't obeying the spirit of the law, and thus they weren't obeying at all. In what ways have you added to God's Word or taken away from it, sidestepping the true issues of the heart? Confess those to God and ask him to cleanse you from the inside out.

October

25

LUKE 9:23-27

*If any of you wants to be my follower, you must give up
your own way, take up your cross daily, and follow me.*

– Luke 9:23

Do you want to find true life? Give up your own way and let me rule in your heart. Take up your cross each day, committing to follow me even if it means you are rejected and persecuted for my sake. Follow me, imitating my example and obeying my commandments.

This path of faithfulness isn't easy, but it is worth it. If you try to save your life, focusing on your own plans and desires, you will lose it in your quest for self-fulfillment. You won't be truly happy, and you will have no part in the heavenly reward that is only found in submitting to me. But if you give up your life for my sake, aligning your priorities with mine, you will gain both eternal life and abundant life now.

The one who is ashamed of me, I will be ashamed of him on judgment day; I will declare that I never knew him. But if you glorify me, I will claim you as my own and share my glory with you. The path of discipleship is a small price to pay for all I give you in return.

It is the irony of the Christian life: Try to hang on to your life and you will lose it, but give up your own way—give up your very life—and you will gain everything in return, abundant life now and forever. Have you made that exchange? Have you given everything to Jesus, or are you trying to hold something back for yourself?

LUKE 14:7-24

Those who exalt themselves will be humbled,
and those who humble themselves will be exalted.

– Luke 14:11

My banqueting table is open to anyone who is humble enough to admit their need. Those who think they deserve the place of honor need not come—there won't be room for them. But anyone who humbles himself or herself before me will be given the best seat in the house.

Don't think you are better than anyone else. You are just a hungry soul who has found the Bread of Life, and now can invite other beggars to the feast. So take to the streets and find the poor, the crippled, the lame, and the blind—for such you were before I saved you. Find those who cannot repay and invite them to the marriage supper of the Lamb.

Think through your day today, and consider when you exalted yourself and when you humbled yourself. What concrete action can you take in the week ahead to pursue humility and give the place of honor to someone else?

October

27

JOHN 1:1-14

To all who believed him and accepted him, he gave the right to become children of God. They are reborn—not with a physical birth resulting from human passion or plan, but a birth that comes from God.

– John 1:12-13

Before anything else, I am. I am the Word who spoke all things into existence. I am the Word who communicates with you, seeking you out and revealing myself to you. I am the Word who took on flesh to show you my glory. I am the Word of life and light.

The world I created became black with sin, and people could no longer see me clearly. And so I, the true light, came into the world to bring light to every person. Just as a lamp illuminates every corner of a dark room, so my glorious presence brings light to every corner of the world.

Many reject me and the life I offer, but anyone who believes in my name becomes my child. I became flesh and dwelt among you to make you my own. Do you believe this?

Jesus' presence brings light that dispels darkness and presents people with a choice. They will either reject him and continue in darkness, or believe him and become his child. Where can you bring Jesus' presence and glory today? As you do so, ask him to bring forth new life in those you minister to.

JOHN 8:31-36

I tell you the truth, everyone who sins is a slave of sin. A slave is not a permanent member of the family, but a son is part of the family forever. So if the Son sets you free, you are truly free.

– John 8:34-36

If you abide in my Word, you are truly my disciple. I will reveal truth to you, and the truth will set you free.

Everyone starts out as a slave of sin—that was your condition at birth. You were powerless to overcome your sinful habits or to serve me, for Satan was the ruler in your heart. But you have become my child through your faith in the death and resurrection of my Son. He has set you free, and now you are no longer enslaved to your desires and temptations. You are my beloved child, and I enable you by my Spirit to obey me.

Live like a free person. Don't give yourself to sin, give yourself to me. Don't live in defeat, claim the victory I have given you over the darkness of Satan. Those sinful habits no longer control you; you can say no to them through my power.

Has Jesus set you free from your slavery to sin? Do your actions and attitudes reflect the reality that you are truly free? If not, ask God to help you disentangle yourself from sin.

JOHN 10:1-21

I am the good shepherd; I know my own sheep,
and they know me, just as my Father knows me and
I know the Father. So I sacrifice my life for the sheep.

– John 10:14-15

I am the gate of the sheep fold, the entrance into true life. It is only by believing in me that you can have eternal life. Anyone who tells you they are the way to eternal life is a thief and a robber, out to steal, kill and destroy. They are trying to rob you of the joy and blessing you have found in me. Don't let them do it!

I am the Good Shepherd, and I gave my life for you. I call you by name and lead you out to safe pasture, to places where you are protected and well fed. I go before you, showing you the right path to take. And you know me intimately: I speak to you constantly so you can distinguish my voice from all the other voices you hear. No one can snatch you away from me, for you are safe forever in my care.

Make a list of all the ways Jesus is a Good Shepherd to you—listing both the general things mentioned in this passage and the more specific ways he has cared for you personally. Thank him for knowing your needs and meeting them.

JOHN 11

*I am the resurrection and the life. Anyone who
believes in me will live, even after dying. Everyone who
lives in me and believes in me will never ever die.*

– John 11:25-26

I am the resurrection and the life. Because you believe in me and trust in me alone to save you, you will live forever. Death is but a temporary separation, a brief sleep, but life with me will never end. The grave cannot hold you, for I defeated death at the Cross.

The life I offer is not just life after death; the life you live now continues on into eternity. Resurrection life is not an abstract truth; it is a living relationship with me that started at the moment you trusted me for salvation and goes on forever. You are already experiencing resurrection life in your soul.

Your time on earth may be brief, but your physical death is the beginning of something far greater: eternity spent face-to-face with me.

Trust me with your days, now and forever.

Read the verses above and imagine Jesus asking you what he asked Martha: "Do you believe this?" Is your belief only mental assent, or do you truly believe it in the deepest core of your being? Ask the Lord to make his resurrection life real to you.

October

31

MATTHEW 18:1-5;
MARK 10:13-16; LUKE 18:15-17

*I tell you the truth, anyone who doesn't receive the
Kingdom of God like a child will never enter it.*

– Mark 10:15

Little children are one of my gifts to you. I delight in their sweet faces and smooth skin just as you do. They are precious to me, so I listen to them and bless them.

Don't look down on youths just because they are not yet fully mature. The simple, trusting, exuberant faith of young people should be imitated and admired. Learn from their example, for the Kingdom of Heaven belongs to those who enter it like a child.

You also have a responsibility to children, to train them up and teach them. Receive them as you would receive me, and don't neglect their care. Tenderly teach them about me and treat them in such a way that it is easy for them to believe I love them.

If you can, spend some time today playing with a child. Enjoy their innocence and humility and enthusiasm. Contemplate what it means to enter the Kingdom like a child, and imagine God smiling at you the same way you smile at them.

November

MATTHEW 19:16-30

It is very hard for a rich person to enter the Kingdom of Heaven. . . . It is easier for a camel to go through the eye of a needle than for a rich person to enter the Kingdom of God!

– Matthew 19:23-24

If you want to see what you truly value, look at how you spend your money. When you store things up for yourself, hoarding what you have and refusing to share with those in need, that is a sign that you don't trust me. You may think your wealth will save you, but in the end it will be eaten by moths, will rust, or be burned in the fire.

When you give your possessions to me, I know that I have your heart. You realize what truly matters—the things that last forever. Generosity is a sign that you trust me to take care of your needs.

In the end, this world and everything in it will pass away. And everything you have comes from my hand; you are merely a steward of it, while I am the owner. So give generously. Don't hold back either your money or your heart.

What do your bank account withdrawals say about your heart? Is your treasure in heaven or on earth? Are you investing in things that last for eternity or in temporary pleasures?

November

2

MATTHEW 20:20-28; MARK 10:35-45

*Whoever wants to be a leader among you must be your servant,
and whoever wants to be first among you must become your
slave. For even the Son of Man came not to be served but to
serve others and to give his life as a ransom for many.*

– Matthew 20:26-28

Even my own people jockey for position, lording any authority I have given them over others. They think they deserve a place of honor, so they work and maneuver to obtain it.

That is not the way of greatness in my Kingdom. Those who want to be great must be the servant of all. Those who give up their position for another, who take last place and treat others as better than themselves, are the ones who will be raised to a place of honor. The last shall be first, and the first shall be last.

So don't strive for a high position here on earth. I'd like to see my people fighting over the positions of lowly service—the food cleanup and the weeding and the diaper changing—for that is what I did for you. I came as a servant of all and gave my life as a ransom for many.

In God's upside-down Kingdom, the way up is the way down; the path to leadership is through service. How could your to-do list and your life goals better reflect these Kingdom priorities?

November

3

MATTHEW 22:34-40; MARK 12:28-34

I know it is important to love him with all my heart and all my understanding and all my strength, and to love my neighbor as myself. This is more important than to offer all of the burnt offerings and sacrifices required in the law.

– Mark 12:33

Some people say faith in me is all about rules and regulations. They complicate it with rituals and lists of commandments.

Sometimes those are helpful tools, but the bottom line to following me is simple. It can be summed up in two commandments: Love me, and love others. Or to put it another way, devote yourself to me with all that you are—heart, soul, mind, and strength. And then live it out by loving those around you as much as you love yourself. Treat them the way you want to be treated. Forgive and be kind to them.

Return to the basics, and you'll see that following me is not complicated—and you can rely on my help to do it.

Sometimes we clog up the Christian life with bunches of dos and don'ts. Our intentions may be good—to be sure we're following God's Word—but we may miss the main thing in the process. Remind yourself today of the beautiful simplicity of the Christian life, and then try to live it out.

MATTHEW 24

No one knows the day or hour when these things will happen,
not even the angels in heaven or the Son himself. Only the Father knows.

– Matthew 24:36

People say they can predict the date of my return, and some even claim to be me. Don't let them lead you astray. No one knows the hour of my return except the Father.

But there will be signs that it is near. There will be wars and rumors of wars as nation rises against nation. There will be famines and earthquakes, great destruction and unrest. Then there will be great suffering for my people, persecution on a level never seen before. People will hate you because you follow me. There will be false christs and false prophets and extreme lawlessness, and many who claimed to know me will fall away.

But you do not need to fear these things, for I will preserve those who are mine. Stand firm to the end. All the words I have spoken will come true. I will return on the clouds of heaven, with power and great glory, and those who have stood firm until the end will meet me in the air and live with me forever.

The list of things that will happen at the end times is scary. But for those who love the Lord, his return is the thing we're eagerly awaiting. It will be for us a day of joy. Take comfort in God's promises to you.

MATTHEW 25

But when the Son of Man comes in his glory, and all the
angels with him, then he will sit upon his glorious throne.

– Matthew 25:31

Be ready for the day of my return, for you do not know when it will
come. Use the time you have to faithfully tell others about the hope
you have in me. Make the most of every opportunity while you still have
time.

When I return in glory, I will sit on my throne and judge each person.
Those who truly know me will be blessed and inherit the Kingdom
prepared for them before the foundation of the world. But those who
only pretended to know me, I will reject.

How can you tell if your heart is mine? Those who truly know me feed
the hungry and welcome strangers in my name. Whatever you do for the
neediest people, those who don't deserve it and cannot repay, you are
doing for me. But if you refuse to minister to those who need your help,
you are rejecting me and don't truly know me.

Put yourself in these stories. Which character do you most
resemble? Are you prepared for Christ's return? Are you investing
what he's given you? Are you serving the "least of these"? Think
of one thing you can do today to invest in eternity, and then do it.

JOHN 14

There is more than enough room in my Father's home. . . .
When everything is ready, I will come and get you,
so that you will always be with me where I am.

– John 14:2-3

Your true home is in heaven with me. That is where you belong, where you will finally feel at peace. I am preparing for you a place near to me, and one day I will come again to take you there. I am the Way, the Truth, and the Life. The only way to the Father—the only way to true, eternal life—is through me.

If you believe this, then you will love me. And if you love me, you will keep my commandments. It won't always be easy, but you are not left alone in the task of obeying me; the Spirit of truth dwells within you to help you. He teaches you all things and helps you remember what is true and right.

Through these promises of a future home in heaven and the Holy Spirit now, I give you peace. Don't let your heart be troubled or afraid; I have promised you eternal life, and I will do it. My presence with you is all you need to face life with courage and peace until that day when you come to be with me forever.

What a comfort it is that God is preparing a home for us in heaven so we can always be with him. Let this truth linger in your heart this day.

JOHN 15:1-11

*Remain in me, and I will remain in you. For a branch
cannot produce fruit if it is severed from the vine,
and you cannot be fruitful unless you remain in me.*

– J o h n   1 5 : 4

I am the vine, my Father is the gardener, and you are the branches—different roles in the natural process of spiritual growth. I am the one who gives life, the one who enables you to grow and become more like me. As long as you remain in me, trusting in me for life and allowing my words to direct you, you will bear spiritual fruit: love, joy, peace, patience, kindness, goodness, faithfulness, gentleness, and self-control.

My Father sanctifies you. He cuts off branches that don't bear fruit. He prunes away parts of your life that are keeping you from bearing as much fruit as you can. He tenderly cares for you and helps you grow in me.

Your only job is to stay attached to me, drawing life from me, and to submit to the pruning process. Stay in my love. Meditate on my Word and do what it says. Apart from me you can do nothing of lasting significance, but with me you can bear much fruit and be filled to overflowing with joy.

Reread these verses and think about the process by which God helps us be more fruitful. Are you fighting that process, grudgingly submitting to it, or trying to facilitate it?

JOHN 15:12-27

This is my commandment: Love each other in the same way I have loved you. There is no greater love than to lay down one's life for one's friends.

– John 15:12-13

I showed you the full extent of love when I laid down my life for you. I showed you how to serve others, and then I died for you even though you were my enemy. Now you are my friend because you love me and do what I command. No one could do more for you than I have.

Here is my command: Love others the same way I have loved you. Serve them. Sacrifice for them. Forgive them, even when they hurt you over and over. Love even those who are your enemies, because I died for you when you were my enemy.

The world will hate you for following me. They will persecute you and say terrible things about you and throw you into prison. But you are not alone. The Holy Spirit is your advocate, speaking the truth into your heart and helping you testify about me to others.

This passage highlights the way God's love for us can flow through us to others. Pray through these verses, thanking God for his friendship to you, and then ask him how you can show his love to those around you.

JOHN 16

*It is best for you that I go away, because if I don't,
the Advocate won't come. If I do go away, then I will send him
to you. And when he comes, he will convict the world of its sin,
and of God's righteousness, and of the coming judgment.*

– J o h n   1 6 : 7 - 8

My disciples wished I would stay on earth. They wanted an earthly kingdom with political power. But my Kingdom is not of this world: It is eternal. And if I hadn't returned to heaven, the Holy Spirit could not have come. It was better for you that I go—that's how important the Holy Spirit's work is.

He is your helper, the one who convicts the world of the sin of rejecting me and makes known to you the righteousness available through faith. He guides you in all truth. Without the Holy Spirit you could not have me in your life.

The Father loves you dearly, and if you ask him anything in my name, you will receive it. Make your prayers bold—I have the power to do anything, and I will do everything that is best. Ask in my name, for my glory, and you will receive with abundant joy.

It's hard to believe it is better for us that Jesus ascended to heaven rather than remaining on earth, but that is the truth. The Holy Spirit's work in our lives is that important. Thank him for living inside you and for his ministry of conviction.

JOHN 17

I pray that they will all be one, just as you and I are one—
as you are in me, Father, and I am in you. And may they
be in us so that the world will believe you sent me.

– John 17:21

This is eternal life: to know me, the only true God, and Jesus Christ, the one I sent to earth. Believe in him, trust him to save you from sin and death, and I will guard and protect your soul for all eternity. You will never be lost.

The world will hate you because you are not one of them. They can tell that you don't belong here; you are a citizen of heaven, a child of light. That doesn't mean you shouldn't engage with the world or love those who are different from you; it just means that your life won't look like theirs because you answer to my call, not your own.

The way my followers treat one another should display to the world who I am. Your love for one another and your unity of mind and heart will show that your true citizenship is in heaven. And it will make people want to have a part in my family as well, because love is attractive and contagious.

These words should touch us deeply because this is Jesus' prayer for us. Make a note of the requests he makes of his Father and the promises he offers us. Which part of this prayer do you most need this week?

ROMANS 1:18-32

Claiming to be wise, they instead became utter fools. And instead of worshiping the glorious, ever-living God, they worshiped idols made to look like mere people and birds and animals and reptiles.

– Romans 1:22-23

Anyone who looks closely at creation can see my eternal power and know innately that there is a God. Yet many people suppress that knowledge so they can go their own way and do anything they want. They refuse to worship me—or, worse, they try to make me in their image.

Suppressing the truth leads to ever-escalating degrees of rebellion and sin. Eventually people become more and more confused. And at some point I let them have their way. I stop showing myself to them and let them do whatever shameful things their hearts desire.

Don't be like them. Let the world I have created draw you into worship. Give me thanks for all I have made, for my goodness to the earth and the mercy I show to all my creatures. When you draw close to me, I will draw close to you.

This passage is heartbreaking, and even more heartbreaking is watching those we love suppress the truth and fall into the clutches of the evil one. Let these words drive you to your knees in prayer for those who are under Satan's influence. Ask God to show himself to them and rescue them.

November

12

ROMANS 5:1-11

God showed his great love for us by sending
Christ to die for us while we were still sinners.

– R o m a n s 5 : 8

When you were utterly helpless, a sinner by birth and my enemy by choice, I came for you. I loved you so much that I died for you to make you my friend, even though you hated me. Now you can rejoice in our new relationship. You have been made right in my sight, and you have peace with me.

This is undeserved privilege, mercy in all its magnificent beauty. You were destined for my wrath, but because I took the punishment you deserved, now you share in my glory.

If you truly understand the magnitude of what I have done for you and the glory that awaits you in heaven, you can rejoice in your problems and trials. You will be glad for them because they develop in you endurance and strength of character. And as I help you through times of suffering, you will grow ever more confident in the hope of your salvation.

A stark contrast to yesterday's reading, here is the gospel in all its beautiful glory. Savor it. Let it marinate in your soul and bring you joy today, even in your problems and trials.

November 13

ROMANS 6:1-14

Since we died with Christ, we know we will also live with him.

– R o m a n s   6 : 8

Because you have joined yourself to Christ in faith, you are united with him in his death and resurrection. You died to sin when he died on the cross, and you were raised to new life when he was raised from the dead. Your old, sinful self was nailed to the cross, and therefore it has no power over you anymore.

Live like a free person! Don't let sin control you. Don't give your body to the powers of darkness to be used as an instrument of evil. Instead, use your whole body to be an instrument of righteousness. My grace has freed you from the power of sin so you can choose to do what is good and right. Give yourself to me and live under the freedom of my grace.

Dead to sin and alive in Christ. Is this how you're living today? Would an outsider notice that sin no longer has control over you? Or are you giving some part of your body as an instrument to serve sin? Live out the truth that you have been raised with Christ, and don't let sin control how you live.

ROMANS 8:1-11

*The Spirit of God, who raised Jesus from the dead, lives in you.
And just as God raised Christ Jesus from the dead, he will give life
to your mortal bodies by this same Spirit living within you.*

– Romans 8:11

At the Cross, I declared an end to sin's control over you and freed you from its grip. You are no longer dominated by the sinful nature, but are instead controlled by the Holy Spirit.

This is great freedom. You can do the things that please me. You can choose actions and attitudes that lead to life and peace. You have living within you the power of Christ, the Spirit who gives you life and makes you right with me. The same power that raised Jesus from the grave now lives within you and gives you true, abundant, resurrection life.

You are no longer a slave, but my dear child. I have adopted you and made you my own. Your soul cries out, "Abba, Father!" and I answer you because you are my child and I am your good Father who loves you and is eager to give you good gifts.

As you go about your day-to-day life, do you have an awareness that you have Holy Spirit power living inside you? How would your life be different if you tapped into his power? What's holding you back from doing so?

November

15

ROMANS 8:18-30

We know that God causes everything to work together for the good of those who love God and are called according to his purpose for them.

– R o m a n s   8 : 2 8

All of creation longs for the day when I will be revealed in all my glory. It groans to be freed from the bondage of death and decay. And you also groan with it—the Holy Spirit gives you a foretaste of the joy that is coming, but you eagerly await your new body as you watch your mortal body fade.

When it seems like the waiting is too long and you may faint under the weight of it all, when your prayers are nothing but desperate, wordless whimpers, the Spirit speaks for you with groans too deep for words—and I answer.

All things work together for your good because you love me. Even your deepest suffering will be redeemed according to my purposes; I will use it to make you more like me. All of the pain and heartache in the world is of little consequence when compared to the joy that is coming. One day you will stand before me in glory, and the pain will fade from your memory as you gaze at my face.

Which of these verses do you most need to hear today? Write it on a slip of paper and then memorize it so you can carry this good news in your heart.

November

16

ROMANS 8:31-39

What shall we say about such wonderful things as these?
If God is for us, who can ever be against us?

– Romans 8:31

I am for you, always and forever at your side. Who would dare to stand against you and accuse you when I have declared that you are in right standing with me? If I even gave you my own Son, won't I also give you everything else? I have chosen you for my own, for Christ died for you and was raised to life for you, and he now stands before me interceding for you.

Therefore, nothing can ever separate you from my love. Even if you have trouble and calamity, you have overwhelming victory in me. Neither death nor life, neither angels nor demons, neither fears nor worries—not even the powers of hell itself—can separate you from my love. You have seen and experienced my love in Christ Jesus, and because of him you have the crown of life.

The beautiful words of Romans 8 truly do leave us speechless. Read them out loud to yourself, speaking them to your soul to give you courage to face anything life throws at you.

ROMANS 12:1-2; 2 CORINTHIANS 6:14-18

Give your bodies to God because of all he has done for you.
Let them be a living and holy sacrifice—the kind he will
find acceptable. This is truly the way to worship him.

– R o m a n s 1 2 : 1

Think on my sacrifice for you, and let it move you to offer your body as a sacrifice to me. Don't copy the behavior and customs of the world, for their ways lead to death. Instead, let me transform your mind and your priorities. Read my Word so you can learn my will, which is good and pleasing and perfect.

You are my temple, for I live in you. How then can you participate in deeds of darkness? What do you have in common with evil now that you have joined yourself to me? Therefore, separate yourself from bad influences, and don't partner with those who do evil.

You are my presence in the world, the way I live among my people until my return. This is a great privilege and responsibility, so take it seriously. Live like my child and share my love with the people I place in your path.

The Old Testament books of Exodus and Leviticus contain a lot of instructions for how sacrifices were to be made. Of course, Jesus was the final, once-for-all sacrifice for sin. In response to his gift of salvation, we should offer ourselves back to him as a sacrifice. What would change about your life if you thought of yourself as a sacrifice to God?

ROMANS 13:1-14

*Everyone must submit to governing authorities.
For all authority comes from God, and those in
positions of authority have been placed there by God.*

– Romans 13:1

I am the Almighty King, and every earthly authority is under my command. I raise up leaders and bring them down to accomplish my purposes. Therefore, honor those who are in authority over you. Do not rebel against what I have instituted, for your leaders are there for your good.

Above all, obey my law to love your neighbor as yourself. Do not do wrong to others. Instead, honor, serve, and love them. Very soon I will return, and you will want to have removed all your deeds of darkness and put on the armor of light. Don't think of ways to indulge your evil desires, but instead clothe yourself with my presence. Then you will live well in the place I have put you and be ready for the day of my return.

According to these verses, how should we respond to a leader we don't like? Should our response be any different than it is to a leader we respect and admire? Think about whether your words, attitudes, and actions toward your leaders are in line with the words of this passage.

ROMANS 14

*Accept other believers who are weak in faith, and don't
argue with them about what they think is right or wrong.*

– R o m a n s   1 4 : 1

You can study and learn what I have clearly outlined in my Word as right or wrong. But about the things I have not commanded, let people live by their own consciences. Let me instruct them. Do not condemn or look down on another believer for their standards in nonessential matters, for each person will stand before my judgment seat and give a personal account.

Live in such a way that you will not cause a brother or sister in the faith to stumble and fall. If their conscience tells them not to eat or drink something, don't eat or drink it in front of them. And if you believe something is wrong, then for you it is sin.

My Kingdom is about living a life of goodness, peace, and joy in the Holy Spirit. Serve me with this attitude, and you will build up the church as you please me. Your priority should be to live rightly before me, not to judge other people on matters of conscience.

What are some things you disagree with other believers about? Are you supporting them in following their conscience? Or are you judging others on nonessential matters of faith? Confess to God the ways in which you might be causing a brother or sister to stumble in their faith, and then work to encourage them.

1 CORINTHIANS 1:18-30

Christ is the power of God and the wisdom of God. This foolish plan of God is wiser than the wisest of human plans, and God's weakness is stronger than the greatest of human strength.

– 1 Corinthians 1:24-25

The very idea that the God of the universe would die on a cross to save the creatures he made, and who had then rebelled against him, is utter madness! The world can't understand it, for no one loves with such scandalous extravagance—no one except me.

This is the power of God, the way I have chosen to bring glory to my name. I am the source of all truth and wisdom. I choose the things the world considers foolish to shame those who think themselves wise. I choose those who are powerless to shame those who are powerful. I choose what is weak and despised by the world to bring to nothing what the world considers important.

You have nothing to boast of in yourself, but you can boast of what I have done: I saved you, and to display my great power and love, I did it in the way the world least expected. Let the one who boasts, boast in me.

Thank God for his wise plan to save sinners through the death and resurrection of Jesus Christ. Then resolve to share this foolish-sounding but infinitely wise Good News with someone today.

1 CORINTHIANS 3:1-23

*You are jealous of one another and quarrel with each
other. Doesn't that prove you are controlled by your sinful
nature? Aren't you living like people of the world?*

– 1 Corinthians 3:3

It's time to grow up and take in solid food. Don't be lazy about your spiritual growth, content to remain a baby in the faith. Your spiritual leaders shouldn't have to spoon-feed you. Read my Word for yourself, meditate on it, and do what it says.

You will know when you've started growing in your faith when you are no longer jealous of other people. You'll be glad for spiritual insight wherever it is found, rather than wishing you had thought of it first. You'll be able to praise me for the blessings I give to others even when I withhold from you something you deeply desire.

True wisdom comes from me. The wisdom of the world is foolishness, so don't place your confidence there. Boast in me; place your confidence in me. I am the one who saves you and causes you to grow in the Spirit.

Many of our churches are often not good reflections of our Savior. We quarrel about the color of the carpeting or the size of the projection screen while ignoring the more urgent task of bringing forth spiritual life and growth. In what ways can you help your church avoid the pitfalls that the Corinthians seem to have fallen into in this passage?

November

22

1 CORINTHIANS 12:1-31

God works in different ways, but it is the
same God who does the work in all of us.

– 1 Corinthians 12:6

My people are supposed to work together as harmoniously as a human body. Each person is needed, and each person has an important role to play. In the same way the body needs hands and feet and internal organs, so my church needs people to serve, people to preach, and people to heal and help.

Just as you would never say, "I don't really need my eye; you can take it out," so also you should never say you don't need the gifts a brother or sister has to offer. Don't belittle the people I have made and the gifts I've given. Each spiritual gift I have given is necessary for the church to be built up and work the way I intend.

Of course, the thing that binds all these gifts together is love, a virtue each person develops as they abide in me. All the talents and spiritual gifts in the world mean nothing if you don't love those around you.

God has given your church everything it needs to bring his light into your community—as long as you're all using your gifts and working together. How can you better use your gifts to serve your church? In what ways can you encourage others to develop and use their gifts?

1 CORINTHIANS 13

Three things will last forever—faith, hope, and love—and the greatest of these is love.

– 1 Corinthians 13:3

Love is the greatest virtue of all, for it is eternal. Without it, you are no more impactful or effective than a noisy gong or clanging cymbal. You may have great gifts of prophecy or faith, but if you don't use them with love, they're of no benefit to you or anyone else.

If you want to see what love looks like, look at me. I came to be the servant of all and to give my life for you. I am patient and kind. I always rejoice in truth. I am always faithful, and my love endures forever.

If you truly love another person, you won't be jealous of their successes or boastful about your own merits or too proud to admit when you're wrong. You'll treat them kindly, without rudeness. You won't demand your own way. You won't be irritable with them. You won't keep a record of the times they've wronged you. You will rejoice whenever truth wins out—even if you're humbled in the process. You will never give up, never lose faith, and always keep hoping for the other person's good. True love endures through every circumstance.

Reread verses 4-7, inserting your name in the place of "love." Which one trips you up? Think of ways you can develop that aspect of your love this week.

1 CORINTHIANS 15:50-58

*Thank God! He gives us victory over sin
and death through our Lord Jesus Christ.*

– 1 Corinthians 15:57

I have swallowed up death. I crushed it once and for all when I rose from the grave, so death can't hold you; its sting has been removed. Through me, you have victory over sin and death!

When all my promises are fulfilled and I return to rule over the new heaven and the new earth, you will need a new body, for your earthly, mortal body can't contain immortal glory. I will give you a body that will never decay or die. In the blink of an eye, at the sound of the last trumpet, you will be transformed into something glorious. Your dying body will be changed into a body that will last forever.

In light of this great hope, be strong. Don't let anyone discourage you or move you from the work I've given you. Live and work for me with enthusiasm, because nothing you do for me is ever useless.

What great hope we have in Jesus! He has defeated sin and death. It can't touch us anymore. Let the joy of this truth help you live today with hope and courage even in the face of death and despair.

2 CORINTHIANS 1:3-11

*The more we suffer for Christ, the more God
will shower us with his comfort through Christ.*

– 2 Corinthians 1:5

When you need tender mercy and a comforting touch, come to me. I will soothe your soul and give you peace as only I can. The more you suffer, the more I can shower you with my peace; the deeper your hurt, the deeper my comfort can reach into your soul.

I am able to comfort you because I suffered for you. I understand your pain because I experienced it too. In the same way, one day you will be able to help others who are going through the same trials you have endured.

When you are crushed beyond your ability to endure, you learn to rely on me. You realize you can't control the things that happen to you, and then you begin to trust me, the one who is always in control. You realize your own strength is feeble and begin to rely on my strength, which never fails. Trust me. I care for you with steadfast love and faithfulness, and I will not waste any of your suffering. Everything you experience I will use for your gain and my glory.

Whom do you know who is crushed today, weighed down with troubles? Maybe it's you. Pray that God would comfort those you know who are hurting so they can in turn comfort others. And think about ways God has comforted you that you can use to help someone else who is going through similar difficulties.

2 CORINTHIANS 4:6-18

*Through suffering, our bodies continue to share in the death of
Jesus so that the life of Jesus may also be seen in our bodies.*

– 2 Corinthians 4:10

My light shines through you, for you know my glory and have seen my face. But you are still a fragile clay jar. I made you needy so everyone would be able to see that your strength comes from my power at work within you. Let me shine my surpassing greatness through the cracked and broken places in your life.

You are pressed by troubles, but not crushed. Perplexed, but not driven to despair. Hunted and tortured, but never abandoned by me. Knocked down, but not destroyed. Your suffering is one way you can share in my death so that my life can be seen in you.

So don't give up or lose heart. Your body may be dying, but your spirit is renewed every day. Your present troubles are small and temporary when compared with the eternal joy of seeing my face forever. Fix your gaze on that future glory, for it vastly outweighs your troubles on earth.

This passage offers us a lot of reason to have hope even when we feel crushed and perplexed and abandoned by God. List all the reasons Paul gave for why we should never give up (verse 16). Keep this list and refer to it on days when life is especially difficult.

2 CORINTHIANS 5:1-10

We know that when this earthly tent we live in is taken down (that is,
when we die and leave this earthly body), we will have a house in heaven,
an eternal body made for us by God himself and not by human hands.

– 2 Corinthians 5:1

Your earthly body will decay and die, for it is only a temporary tent for your soul. Your true home is in heaven, where you will have an eternal body that I am making for you.

Your earthly body is groaning and sighing, failing by the day, and you long for something more permanent. Take heart, one day your weak flesh will be swallowed up by a new, living body that can never die. Death is swallowed up in life—that is my promise to you.

Put your confidence in these truths and let them give you courage in the face of death. Everything you see and experience here on earth will soon pass away, but your life in me is forever. Rest in these truths, for that is what it means to live by faith, not by sight.

What would be different about your day if you lived by believing rather than seeing (verse 7)? Ask God for a fresh vision of the joy that awaits you in heaven and for an eternal perspective on the cares of this day.

GALATIANS 3:7, 26–4:7

Because we are his children, God has sent the Spirit of his
Son into our hearts, prompting us to call out, "Abba, Father."
Now you are no longer a slave but God's own child.
And since you are his child, God has made you his heir.

– Galatians 4:6-7

Each person who cries out to me in faith for salvation, I abundantly save. I not only free them from slavery to sin, I also make them my own child. I adopt them into my family and love them as my own. The externals do not matter in my Kingdom—every nationality, man or woman, slave or free, each one becomes my true child.

And not just my child, but my heir, my favored child and the recipient of my blessing. Each one—even the one who was saved from a life of utter depravity—will receive all the promises I have made to the children of Abraham and share in my glory for all eternity.

As proof of your adoption, I have given you my Spirit. Through him I live in you and prompt you to cry out to me. You have every right to cry out to me, "Abba, Father!" And just as any good earthly father does, I love it when you come to me with all of your joys and sorrows.

Do you sometimes wonder if you're really saved, if God really loves you? We don't have to wonder—we have proof that we are God's children, heirs to all his promises. The Holy Spirit living inside us gives us love for God and a desire to please him. If you have the urge to cry out to God as your Father, that is the Holy Spirit proving to you that you belong to God.

GALATIANS 5:1-16

*Let the Holy Spirit guide your lives. Then you
won't be doing what your sinful nature craves.*

– Galatians 5:16

I have made you free. The law had enslaved you, forcing you to obey its regulations and pointing out all your failures. It could not save you, for you could never be holy apart from me. But now I have met all those requirements to free you from its grip. What you could not do for yourself, I did for you.

Live as a free person! Don't allow yourself to get tied up again in slavery to the law by trying to earn your salvation. You know that salvation is through faith, my righteousness imputed to you. You are called to freedom, not slavery.

That doesn't mean you should satisfy your sinful nature. No, the freedom I have given you is freedom to serve one another in love, freedom to obey me, freedom to choose to do what is right rather than being shackled to your sin.

People think they will be happy if they give in to their every desire and whim, but really that is slavery to sin and self. True freedom is being able to say no to your sinful cravings and yes to God. Are you living out the freedom that is yours in Christ?

GALATIANS 5:16-25

*Those who belong to Christ Jesus have nailed the passions and desires
of their sinful nature to his cross and crucified them there. Since we are
living by the Spirit, let us follow the Spirit's leading in every part of our lives.*

– Galatians 5:24-25

If you let my Spirit lead you, you won't be doing what your sinful nature craves. Apart from me, you want to do evil things—you are filled with sexual immorality, impurity, lust, idolatry, quarreling, jealousy, angry outbursts, selfish ambition, and dissension. These deeds of darkness leave you feeling ashamed and empty. But with me, you are free from all that. Your old sinful nature was nailed to the cross, and you don't have to give in to its demands anymore.

As you abide in me, you will be more and more controlled by the Spirit. You will grow in love, joy, peace, patience, kindness, goodness, faithfulness, gentleness, and self-control. Your desires will be transformed so that you will long to do good rather than evil. Each part of your life will increasingly overflow with good, Spirit-filled characteristics as you submit to my work in you.

The more we submit to the Holy Spirit's work in our lives, the more of our lives are characterized by God's desires and God's heart for others. Are you holding back some part of your life, hoping God doesn't notice? Give it to him and let him fill you with his light and life.

December

EPHESIANS 1:1-10

All praise to God, the Father of our Lord Jesus Christ,
who has blessed us with every spiritual blessing in the
heavenly realms because we are united with Christ.

– Ephesians 1:3

I don't hold back anything from you; every spiritual blessing is yours in Christ. I chose you before the foundation of the world, that you would know me and be made holy. I predestined you for adoption as my own child. This is my will, my urgent purpose.

I have lavished upon you all the benefits of my loving character—redemption, forgiveness, and rich grace. And I have revealed to you the mystery of my will to reconcile to myself people from every nation. I have not kept back any secrets of my goodness and love.

Now live as the blessed person that you are. You have everything in me; don't pine away for earthly things that don't last. You are my dear child; don't doubt my love for you.

Make a list of "every spiritual blessing" that is described in these verses. Next to each one, write a practical implication that blessing has in your life.

EPHESIANS 1:11-14

The Spirit is God's guarantee that he will give us the inheritance he promised and that he has purchased us to be his own people. He did this so we would praise and glorify him.

– Ephesians 1:14

Your eternal inheritance in me is secure. I planned from the beginning of time that you would be part of my Kingdom, one of my own. It was my will for all eternity to make you my treasured possession.

As a down payment on your eternal inheritance, I have given you the Holy Spirit. His empowering presence in your life guarantees that you are mine, and that everything I have promised is yours. He is the one who protects and preserves you until your faith becomes sight.

Live with courage as you anticipate the day when you will see me face-to-face. No one can snatch you out of my hand; the Holy Spirit ensures that. Nor are you ever apart from me, for I live in you. Live each day to the praise of my glory with the Holy Spirit's help.

Do you often think about the Holy Spirit's presence in your life? Spend time today thinking about all the things he does for you— convicting of sin, empowering you to obey God, guaranteeing God's promises, and giving you comfort and peace. Thank God for the amazing gift of the Spirit living inside you.

December

3

EPHESIANS 1:15-23

I pray that your hearts will be flooded with light so that you can understand the confident hope he has given to those he called—his holy people who are his rich and glorious inheritance.

– Ephesians 1:18

As each day you look to me, I open the eyes of your heart so you can know in the depths of your soul the hope I have called you to. I give you a spirit of wisdom and knowledge so you can understand my calling and the riches of the glorious inheritance you have in me. I give you hope and joy that lasts forever.

This is the immeasurable greatness of my power at work within you. I change you from the inside out. The same power that raised Jesus from the dead and seated him at my right hand is now living inside you. My fullness fills you.

All of this is yours—and you can tap into it any time by reading my Word and talking to me.

These words are Paul's prayer for the church at Ephesus. Pray them for the people on your prayer list today. How does praying for these spiritual things differ from the things you usually pray about? How can you regularly incorporate Paul's example into your prayer life?

December

4

EPHESIANS 2:1-10

We are God's masterpiece. He has created us anew in Christ Jesus,
so we can do the good things he planned for us long ago.

– Ephesians 2:10

If you need evidence of how great your need for me is, consider this—before I came into your life, you were spiritually dead. No heartbeat, no signs of life, just complete deadness. You lived for your passions and were destined for my wrath.

But then my mercy broke through and gave you life. You were dead in sin and I made you alive with Christ. You are now raised up with him, seated in the heavenly places in Christ Jesus. This is all my work, all grace. There is nothing you could do to save yourself; it is only because of the riches of my grace in kindness toward you that you now have everlasting life.

My work did not end there—I created you for good works. I am still in the process of sanctifying you and helping you grow. This, too, is grace. Don't give up on yourself; I am still at work in and through you.

We all love a good before-and-after picture. This passage shows us what we were before Christ saved us, and what we are now. On a piece of paper, write "before" and "after" columns, listing each characteristic. Thank Jesus for this transformation.

EPHESIANS 2:11-22

We are carefully joined together in him, becoming a holy temple for the Lord.

– Ephesians 2:21

Here is what you were: Separated from me. Alienated from the community of believers. A stranger to the covenant of my promise. Without hope and without God. Utterly alone and rejected, far from me and an enemy of my grace.

But now, through my blood sacrifice, I have brought you near. I am your peace, and I have broken down the wall of hostility that you built between us by your rebellion. I have reconciled you to myself through my sacrifice on the cross. You have hope, for you have me. Now you are my beloved child and I am your Abba, Father. Our relationship is open and free. You have no need to feel shame or anxiety, for we are at peace.

Not only do you have me—you have a spiritual family as well. You are a member of my household, built on the foundation of the apostles and prophets. Together you are a holy temple, a dwelling place for me by the Spirit. You have a place to belong, mothers and fathers and sisters and brothers in the faith to look after you and care for you.

The cross of Christ unifies people from every background, race, status, and socioeconomic circumstance. Find a believer you can connect with whom you wouldn't normally interact with, and see what you can learn from him or her.

EPHESIANS 3:14-21

*May you have the power to understand, as all God's people should,
how wide, how long, how high, and how deep his love is. May you
experience the love of Christ, though it is too great to understand fully.*

– Ephesians 3:18-19

I have created you and given you a special identity in me. Draw from the riches of my glory so that you may be strong. Let my Spirit empower your inner being and dwell in your heart through faith.

If you live in me in this way, you will be rooted and grounded in my love. You will have strength to comprehend the breadth and length and height and depth of my love for you, a love that surpasses understanding, and it will give you stability in an ever-changing world. You will be filled with all of my fullness, nothing held back.

I am able to do this—and more—through my power at work within you. Indeed, I can do far more abundantly than all you ask or imagine. Let my glorious presence fill you more and more each day so you can see how loved you are and be empowered to respond to me in faith.

Have you experienced the love of Jesus as Paul described it in these verses? Ask him to implant it deep in your heart today.

EPHESIANS 4:1-16

Be patient with each other, making allowance for each other's faults because of your love. Make every effort to keep yourselves united in the Spirit, binding yourselves together with peace.

– E p h e s i a n s   4 : 2 - 3

You have a calling: to follow me. Now walk in that calling. Imitate me by being humble and gentle. Patiently bear with one another in love, just as I patiently bear with your failings. Be eager to maintain unity and peace.

All of my followers make up one body, and you are indwelt by one Spirit. You have the same hope and the same calling. You serve the same Lord and share the same faith and baptism. I the Lord am one—one God who is over all and through all and in all.

But there is great diversity in my body. Each part, each person with the talents I have given them, is needed. As each person uses his or her gifts and appreciates the gifts of everyone else, the body works together to fulfill my purposes in the world. So build one another up in love. Share your gifts with others and ask them to share theirs.

Our unity in the body of Christ has as its foundation the Holy Spirit. It is not based on our abilities or preferences. As long as we are trying to keep in step with the Spirit and making allowance for one another's faults, we will be unified.

December

8

EPHESIANS 4:17-32

Let the Spirit renew your thoughts and attitudes. Put on your new nature, created to be like God—truly righteous and holy.

– Ephesians 4:23-24

You don't have as much in common with your unbelieving neighbors as you used to. They are hopelessly confused, and their minds are full of darkness. They have closed their minds and hardened their hearts against me, and as a result they have no sense of shame. They live for their lustful pleasures.

That isn't who you are anymore. You know the truth, so throw off your old sinful nature. Let my Spirit renew your thoughts and attitudes. Start living as you were meant to—becoming more righteous and holy with each passing day.

Stop telling lies; instead speak the truth. Don't let anger control you; instead be controlled by my Spirit. Don't use foul or abusive language; instead speak words that are good and helpful. Get rid of bitterness and rage; instead be kind to each other, tenderhearted and forgiving.

As you get dressed each morning this week, imagine yourself putting on the new nature that is yours in Christ. You no longer have to live in shame and lust and deception as you used to; now you can be forgiving and generous and holy.

EPHESIANS 5:1-19

*Imitate God, therefore, in everything you do, because
you are his dear children. Live a life filled with love, following
the example of Christ. He loved us and offered himself
as a sacrifice for us, a pleasing aroma to God.*

– Ephesians 5:1-2

You've seen how little boys like to follow their daddies around and imitate them. They try on Daddy's giant shoes and pretend to go to work just like him. That is how you should act toward me. Imitate what I do, for you are my beloved child and I am your dear Father.

Walk in love. Give yourself up for those around you, in the same way I gave myself up as a sacrifice for you. Do what is good and right and true. Submit to others out of reverence for me.

Walk in light, for you are a child of the light. Act in such a way that you do not need to hide or be ashamed. Stay away from the filthy talk and sexual immorality and impurity of the people who are still in darkness. Instead, be thankful. Speak in psalms and hymns and spiritual songs, singing and making melody with a thankful heart.

As you read your Bible and listen to Bible teaching this week, look for ways you can imitate God. Are you making the most of every opportunity to follow his example?

December
10

EPHESIANS 6:10-18

Put on all of God's armor so that you will be
able to stand firm against all strategies of the devil.

– Ephesians 6:11

Y ou are in a battle, not against flesh and blood but against the rulers and cosmic powers of evil. The threat is more serious than if you were fighting mere mortals. But I have not left you defenseless.

I have given you armor to put on. Fasten the belt of truth around your waist. Affix the righteousness of Christ across your chest like a breastplate. Shod your feet with the gospel of peace so you can share it with others. Shield yourself with your faith and put on the helmet of salvation. Your only offensive weapon is my Word, so wield it carefully. It is able to divide soul and spirit, joints and marrow.

As you go into battle, know that I am with you. Pray in the Spirit as you fight, and then let me fight for you. In this way you can face the evil day with courage and stand firm no matter what assaults may come against your faith.

God supplies the power to fight against evil, but we have to put on the armor. Reread the passage and imagine yourself putting on each piece. Thank God for giving you everything you need to fight the evil forces in the world.

PHILIPPIANS 2:1-11

Don't be selfish; don't try to impress others. Be humble, thinking
of others as better than yourselves. Don't look out only for
your own interests, but take an interest in others, too.

– P h i l i p p i a n s   2 : 3 - 4

As you look at the fighting and quarrels between believers, unity in the church can seem like an elusive dream. Here is the secret—follow my example of humility, and you will soon discover that you and your spiritual brothers and sisters have the same mind.

I have provided the ultimate example of humility: I am God, yet instead of holding tightly to my rightful position, I gave it all up. I made myself nothing, taking on the form of a servant and putting on human flesh. The Creator of all took on all the limits of his creatures. And I obeyed the Father even to death on a cross.

Are you willing to follow my example? You are a mere creature, so it is not a big step down for you to become a servant. But the benefits of doing so are immense. Give up your rivalry and conceit. Consider others better than yourself and look out for their interests rather than your own. Follow me in humility, and you will find unity.

What can you do to bring unity to your church this week? To your family? Ask God to show you how to follow the example of Christ's humility and self-sacrifice.

PHILIPPIANS 3:7-21

*Everything else is worthless when compared with the infinite value
of knowing Christ Jesus my Lord. For his sake I have discarded
everything else, counting it all as garbage, so that I could gain Christ.*

– Philippians 3:8

Accounts work differently in my Kingdom. The things that seem to matter so much on earth—position, power, and prestige—are as worthless as sewage. The people who strive after these things are headed toward destruction. Their god is their belly, and they glory in their shame.

The surpassing treasure you long for is found in knowing me, in discovering you have been credited with my righteousness and are an heir of eternal life. This is what truly matters in life and in death.

Now that you have gained me and have a righteousness that comes through faith, press on to make this your own. Forget the things you used to think mattered so much and strain forward into my calling. Set your mind on things above, for your citizenship is in heaven. Look forward to that day when your lowly body will be transformed into a glorious, immortal one.

Do you think of everything else in life as worthless compared with the value of knowing Christ? Contemplate everything he has done for you, perhaps reviewing Ephesians 2 as a reminder, and ask him to so fill your vision with himself that everything in this world pales in comparison.

December
13

PHILIPPIANS 4:4-9

Always be full of joy in the Lord. I say it again—rejoice!
- Philippians 4:4

You do not need to be anxious about anything. When you are tempted to worry, simply pray. Bring everything before me—even the little things, for if it concerns you, then I want to hear about it and give you my perspective on it. And be sure to offer your prayers with thankfulness.

Guard your mind with honorable thoughts. Think about things that are worthy of praise, lovely, and commendable. Fill your mind with my greatness so that you can have the right perspective on life.

If you do these things, my peace will rule in your heart, for I will guard you from anxiety. Even when every circumstance tells you to be afraid, I will give you peace in your inmost being. The secret to peace and joy is to choose thankfulness, pray about everything, and guard your mind.

Do you want more joy? Are you often prone to depression? Use the advice in these verses to reshape your attitude. Think of practical ways you can discipline yourself to be prayerful, grateful, and at peace.

COLOSSIANS 1:15-23

He has reconciled you to himself through the death of Christ in his physical body. As a result, he has brought you into his own presence, and you are holy and blameless as you stand before him without a single fault.

– Colossians 1:22

I created all things, in heaven and on earth, visible and invisible, thrones and rulers and authorities—all things were created by me and for me, and I hold it all together by my powerful word. I am the head of the church, the firstborn from the dead, the beginning and the end.

You had no hope of knowing me, but in mercy I reconciled all things to myself by the blood of the Cross. You were once alienated from me, hostile toward me and full of evil. But now you are holy and blameless and above reproach before me. I have made you beautiful. This is the hope of the gospel.

These truths are simple but profound. Continue in the faith, reminding yourself daily of these truths and living them out.

Repeat Colossians 1:15-20 as a hymn of praise. How can meditating on these truths help you live differently today?

COLOSSIANS 1:24-29

*I am glad when I suffer for you in my body, for I am participating
in the sufferings of Christ that continue for his body, the church.*

– Colossians 1:24

Just as I suffered for you, you may one day be called to suffer for me. In that day you can rejoice that you have been counted worthy to suffer for my name. I was afflicted for you, and you are blessed if you suffer for me and for my body, the church.

When you suffer for me, I am glorified. Let your actions and words communicate the mystery of the Cross. Declare the riches of the hope of glory that is in you. In this way you will fulfill the work I have given you, and people will see your example and grow in their faith.

The strength and energy for this task does not come from you, it comes from me. Likewise, in your own strength you do not have the ability to endure suffering with joy, but I will help you. So rely on the energy I powerfully work within you as you work for me today.

We tend to avoid suffering—and even mild discomfort—whenever we can. How might the idea of participating in the sufferings of Christ help you be more willing to make sacrifices, as Paul did, for the spread of the gospel?

COLOSSIANS 2:6-15

*Just as you accepted Christ Jesus as your Lord, you must
continue to follow him. Let your roots grow down into him,
and let your lives be built on him. Then your faith will grow strong
in the truth you were taught, and you will overflow with thankfulness.*

– Colossians 2:6-7

Establish yourself in the truth. Remind yourself of it, so you will continually abound in thanksgiving for all I have done for you.

Here is the truth about who you are: When you were buried with me in baptism, I raised you up in faith. You were dead in sin, and I made you alive in me. You were guilty and rebellious, but I forgave all your trespasses. I cancelled the record of debt and the legal demands that you could not meet. I nailed it all to the cross and silenced your accuser.

Now, walk in the freedom I have given you. Don't be a slave to your old, sinful nature or the old laws that condemned you. Don't add to or subtract from the finished work of salvation. Obey me, rooted and built up in the faith and trusting in me alone to save you.

Are there any things you did when you first became a Christian that you no longer do? Maybe you read your Bible more often, or you went to church and Bible study regularly but you've let it slide. Whatever you used to do to grow in Christ, return to those habits.

December

17

COLOSSIANS 3:1-17

Since you have been raised to new life with Christ,
set your sights on the realities of heaven, where Christ
sits in the place of honor at God's right hand.

– C o l o s s i a n s   3 : 1

Your actions and priorities should reflect your true identity as my child. If you've been raised up with Christ, your mind should be focused on me, for your true life is in heaven with me. The desires and priorities that the world tells you are important should no longer matter to you.

Put to death what belongs to your old life: sexual immorality, passion, evil desire, and covetousness. Don't let anger or wrath or obscenity have any part in your life. Live in complete honesty before me and before others.

Clothe your new self as befits someone who is holy and beloved, chosen by me. Live with compassion, kindness, humility, meekness, and patience. Bear with each other in love. Forgive as I have forgiven you. Let love cover over your relationships. Allow my peace to rule in your heart, affecting everything you do. Be thankful, and let my Word fill you.

What fills your mind and grabs your attention? What do you spend the most time and energy thinking about and planning for? Is your mind set on Christ, or on the things of this world? What do your priorities say about your heart?

1 THESSALONIANS 4:13–5:11

Since we believe that Jesus died and was raised to life
again, we also believe that when Jesus returns, God will
bring back with him the believers who have died.

– 1 Thessalonians 4:14

Those who know me, the resurrection and the life, need not grieve without hope. You know that I died and rose again, and that I have promised to bring those who know me to glory. Indeed, those who die in this life will see me before those who are still alive at my return.

It is an indisputable fact: I will return, with a cry of command, with the voice of an archangel, with the trumpet of God. Encourage your brothers and sisters in the faith with this truth.

The timing of my return is known only to God. It will come when you least expect it, so be ready for it at any time. Keep your affairs in order so you will have no regrets when I appear. But don't fear the day of my return—for you it is the consummation of your salvation, a day of pure joy.

Twice in these verses Paul tells us to encourage one another with reminders of Christ's return (verses 4:18, 5:11). When was the last time you talked with someone about heaven? Think of a way to weave it into your conversation today, and be encouraged as you do so that Jesus is coming soon!

December

19

2 TIMOTHY 2:14-26

> *Work hard so you can present yourself to God and receive his approval. Be a good worker, one who does not need to be ashamed and who correctly explains the word of truth.*
>
> – 2 Timothy 2:15

Do you long for my approval? Then do your best to obey my Word. You have been cleansed from sin and set apart for my holy work, so do it with excellence. Use all the training and resources available to you to correctly interpret and teach my Word.

Don't get drawn into irreverent babbling and foolish quarrels, for such things lead to decay in the body of Christ. Flee youthful passions and run after righteousness, faith, love, and peace. Pursue these virtues like the treasures they are.

My servants should be kind, able to teach, and willing to patiently endure evil. When you must correct wrong teaching, do it with gentleness so your hearers are led into repentance and knowledge of the truth.

Would God approve of your words, or do they cause you shame? Paul offered some advice here for how we can use our words well so that we are good workers who correctly explain the Word of Truth. Find one takeaway from this passage that you can put into practice this week.

December

20

2 TIMOTHY 3:1-7, 14-17

*All Scripture is inspired by God and is useful to teach us what is true and
to make us realize what is wrong in our lives. It corrects us when
we are wrong and teaches us to do what is right. God uses it
to prepare and equip his people to do every good work.*

– 2 Timothy 3:16-17

These last days are full of difficulty. People love themselves, love money, and love pleasure. They are proud and ungrateful, lacking self-control. Worst of all are the hypocrites, those who take on the appearance of godliness but deny its power. These people attempt to lead you astray.

Don't let them influence you. Continue in the sound teaching you have received. Keep on in your study of my Word, which is able to make you understand salvation. Don't stop believing what you know is true.

Every part of the Bible is straight from my mouth. It will teach you, correct you when you go astray, and train you in righteousness. Read my Word and you will be equipped and ready for every good work.

Reading through this description of people in the last days is almost like reading the news updates on our phones—this is what we're living through right now. What does Paul encourage us to do in order to live well in the midst of a world where everyone loves themselves, scoffs at the things of God, and hates what is good?

December
21

TITUS 3:3-11

When God our Savior revealed his kindness and love,
he saved us, not because of the righteous things we had done,
but because of his mercy. He washed away our sins,
giving us a new birth and new life through the Holy Spirit.

– Titus 3:4-5

Here is what you were: foolish, disobedient, fickle, easily led astray, a slave to your passions and pleasures, full of hate . . .

But I changed everything. My goodness and loving-kindness drew you to me. In my mercy, I washed you clean and justified you. You are now a beloved child, an heir of my glory, the recipient of the certain hope of eternal life.

This is all my work; you could not do it for yourself. If you need proof of that, just remember what you were without me. Your salvation doesn't rely on you—it relies on me. I saved you not because of your righteousness, but because of my own. Therefore you can be sure that you are mine, and all of my promises will come to pass.

Meditate on God's kindness and love as it's described in this passage, and then think about how you can demonstrate the mind of Christ to those around you.

December
22

HEBREWS 4:14-16; 6:19-20; 7:26-28; 10:19-23

By his death, Jesus opened a new and life-giving
way through the curtain into the Most Holy Place.

– Hebrews 10:20

I am your Great High Priest, and the way of forgiveness that I offer is far greater than that of any earthly priest. I became human, like you in every respect. I can understand the trials and temptations of your life because I lived them too.

But unlike you, I am without sin. I am holy, innocent, unstained—and I offered myself in your place. My death on the cross accomplished what no one else could do; it gave you complete forgiveness. The sacrifice I offered was a once-for-all perfect sacrifice, able to save for all eternity those who place their faith in me for salvation.

Do you believe this? Then come, enter boldly into my presence and you will find mercy and grace. I have torn down the separation between us with my flesh. You can have full assurance of faith, a firm anchor for your soul, because I am the Great High Priest who has washed you clean. Your faith and your forgiveness rest on me, not on you, and therefore they are sure and certain.

In the Old Testament, the high priest went before God and mediated on behalf of his sinful people. Now we can go to God ourselves. Think about this gift you've been given to enter into the holy place, God's throne room, and then take full advantage of that gift today by spending time with him.

December
23

HEBREWS 12:3-13; JAMES 1:2-4, 12

*As you endure this divine discipline, remember
that God is treating you as his own children.*

– Hebrews 12:7

Are you suffering? Do you have trials of various kinds? Choose joy. Be thankful for the hardships. These things test your faith and make you steadfast in me. They prove that your confidence is resting in me, not in yourself. When you have come through, your faith will be complete and you will receive the crown of life.

No one likes to be disciplined, but good parents discipline their children for their own good. It is not loving to let someone continue on the wrong path. And I am the best parent, who loves you far more than any earthly father ever could. When I discipline you, I am treating you as a dear child.

So press on. Be thankful that I am working for your good, and let my work lead to holiness in your life. If you submit to my work, one day you will enjoy the peaceful fruit of righteousness.

When you think back over the past year, do you see any ways God has disciplined you? What growth has occurred as a result? Thank him for loving you as his child, even when the discipline hurts.

December 24

JAMES 2:14-26

*What good is it, dear brothers and sisters, if you say you have faith
but don't show it by your actions? Can that kind of faith save anyone?*

– James 2:14

You can't have faith without works. Or to put it another way, works without faith are dead acts of hypocrisy, and faith without works is not faith at all. Abraham was saved by his faith, but his faith was proved when he offered Isaac on the altar. Just as the body apart from the spirit is dead, so also faith without action is dead.

If you truly believe in me, your faith will naturally lead to good works. You will be so grateful for all I have done for you that you will want to serve me in return.

So don't hold back from doing good to others. Let your gratitude toward me overflow into love and kindness toward others. In this way your faith will bear fruit.

Think about the things you spend time and money on. Does your lifestyle reflect your faith? If not, what kinds of ministries might you get involved in for the coming year?

2 PETER 1:3-11

By his divine power, God has given us
everything we need for living a godly life.

– 2 Peter 1:3

If you know me, you have everything you need for life and godliness. You know you are called, and that I have given you great and precious promises. You know I have given you a new nature, incorruptible and destined for eternal life with me. You know your true identity lies with me.

In light of these truths, add to your faith virtue, knowledge, self-control, steadfastness, and godliness. And over all these things put on love. Don't settle for tiny faith—work toward spiritual growth. Live out the truth of who you are in me, for you have everything you need to obey me.

If you have these qualities in ever-increasing amounts, you won't be ineffective or unfruitful as a Christian. You will remember where you've come from and where you're going, and that will determine how you live each day.

God has given us everything we need to grow in him. We have the time, resources, and power to live a godly life. Do you believe this promise, or are you waiting for something to happen before you start growing? Take hold of everything God has given you and start to grow in him.

REVELATION 2:2-7; 3:1-6

I have this complaint against you. You don't
love me or each other as you did at first!

— Revelation 2:4

I see everything you do—nothing is hidden from me. I see the way you patiently endure trials and all the times you stand up to temptation and overcome. I also see the way you faithfully test and root out false teachers. You are tireless in this task. An outsider would say you have it all together, that you are piously devoted to me.

Yet something is missing. You do all the right things out of habit and duty, not out of love. You are dead inside. The love you had for me at first has grown dim. You have lost your first love.

It's not too late: fan it into flame. Remember what you did when you first knew me, when the bloom of love was fresh, and do those things again. Return to me and to the love we used to have. Nurture your relationship with me the same way happily married couples nurture their romance.

Have you ever been in love? If so, think of how you felt in those early weeks. You wanted to be with that person all the time. You savored their every word and action. Apply those same feelings and actions to your relationship with God.

December
27

REVELATION 2:8-11; MATTHEW 10:16-25

Don't be afraid of what you are about to suffer. The devil will throw some of you into prison to test you. You will suffer for ten days. But if you remain faithful even when facing death, I will give you the crown of life.

– R e v e l a t i o n   2 : 1 0

As my coming gets closer, you will experience increased persecution. People will slander you and throw you into prison. They will drag you into court and spread lies about you. If they did these things to me, it should not surprise you when they also do them to those who are called by my name.

But don't fear; I will be with you. You don't even need to strategize and plan your words, for I will give you the words to say at just the moment you need to say them. Indeed, I will speak my words through you. And in the end, I will be glorified through your words and your suffering.

Stand firm to the end. Endure this suffering and you will receive the crown of life, and it will all be worth it.

Believers in many parts of the world are suffering persecution as described in these verses. You may be next. Pray for those who are persecuted, that they will endure firm to the end, and trust God to take care of you when you are persecuted.

REVELATION 3:14-22

Look! I stand at the door and knock. If you hear my voice and open the door, I will come in, and we will share a meal together as friends.

– Revelation 3:20

You think your riches can save you, that you don't need me. But you are wretched, pitiable, poor, blind, and naked without me. You think your good works can save you, but they are nothing more than lukewarm deeds of convenience, designed to look pious but not cost you too much. You're trying to wash yourself clean, when only my white garments of salvation can save you.

Those whom I love, I discipline. With these harsh but tender words I am calling you back to the path of life. Behold, I am standing at the door of your heart and knocking. If you open the door, I will come in and eat with you. We will be friends. Each day I make this offer of close relationship; don't shut me out.

This is the time of year when many people invite friends and family over to celebrate. As you invite guests in and are yourself a guest, invite Jesus to come in both to your fellowship with others and the quietness of your own heart.

December
29

REVELATION 19; EPHESIANS 5:22-29

Blessed are those who are invited to the wedding feast of the Lamb.

– Revelation 19:9

You are indeed blessed, for you have been invited to the wedding feast of the Lamb. The bride, my church, is ready—adorned for me, spotless and lovely. I am faithful and true, and I have done the work to present you to myself holy, without any blemish or wrinkle.

This is why I came, why I died for you, why I love and nourish and cherish you: Because one day we will enter into the most intimate relationship possible. I came to you and gave up everything to make you my beautiful bride.

This is why you also must love and nourish and cherish the church: Because they are part of you, and you are part of them. The life I offer you in heaven, where you will live with me, is for all my people. So don't neglect the church. Give of yourself for her welfare, just as I gave myself to help the whole church be ready for the day of my return.

You have been invited to the best party of all—the marriage supper for Christ and his church. Even as you celebrate this season of festivity, look forward to that day, which will be far better than anything we can imagine.

REVELATION 21

He will wipe every tear from their eyes, and there will be no more death or sorrow or crying or pain. All these things are gone forever.

– Revelation 21:4

I am coming soon, and when I do, you will see the new heaven and the new earth. In the day when I return, my home will be among my people. I will live with you, and you will be mine. All your hopes will be reality; everything you ever wanted and more will come true, for my presence is the greatest treasure you could long for.

When I return, all things will be restored to the perfection for which they were created. There will be no need for sun or moon, for my glory will give light. Whenever you are thirsty, you will drink freely from the springs of the water of life.

I will wipe every tear from your eyes, and there will be no more death or sorrow or crying or pain. The hardships of life will fade in your remembrance until they are completely gone. Your first glimpse of me sitting on my throne, making everything new, will banish every sorrow from your memory. This is the future that is coming for you. Take heart as you wait for that day.

Let these promises of heaven enter deep into your soul today. This is the Good News we live and share with others, the culmination of our entire existence. And it is assured.

December

31

REVELATION 22

*I am the Alpha and the Omega, the First
and the Last, the Beginning and the End.*

– Revelation 22:13

I am the Alpha and the Omega, the First and the Last, the Beginning and the End. I am the bright morning star, the source of all light and truth. In the end, when everything else is stripped away, there I am—just as I was before time began.

I say to you, "Come." If you are thirsty, come and drink freely of the water of life. Eat your fill from the tree of life—refreshment from my abundance. Be healed, once for all time.

Come before me and gaze at my face, for my name is written on your forehead, declaring that you are mine. The curse of sin is lifted, and you will live in my light forever. You will be with me and reign with me. This is what you've been waiting for. I am coming soon—amen, let it be so!

This verse is really the summary of everything you've been reading and thinking about this year as you've used this devotional guide. Jesus is everything—everything that matters and everything you need. Worship him.